Self-Guided Exposure and Response Prevention Therapy for OCD

Self-Guided Exposure and Response Prevention Therapy for OCD

A Compassionate Workbook for Obsessive-Compulsive Disorder

NATALIA AÍZA, LPC, MA

Zeitgeist · New York

Content Warning
This book discusses OCD fears related to violence, abuse, and self-harm, which some readers may find upsetting. If you are in distress, please do not hesitate to reach out for support. In the United States, call 988 or text "TALK" to 741741 to connect with a crisis counselor. You are not alone.

Zeitgeist™
An imprint and division of Penguin Random House LLC
1745 Broadway, New York, NY 10019
zeitgeistpublishing.com
penguinrandomhouse.com

ISBN: 9798217150878

Printed in the United States of America
1st Printing

Interior illustrations © by Shutterstock.com
Cover photograph © by Akela/Stocksy
Book design by Katy Brown
Author photograph © by Matthew Williams Photography
Edited by Clara Song Lee

The authorized representative in the EU for product safety and compliance is Penguin Random House Ireland, Morrison Chambers, 32 Nassau Street, Dublin D02 YH68, Ireland. https://eu-contact.penguin.ie

To Nydia, who has helped me be
brave since we were 16.
I am in awe of your strength.

Contents

Part Two: Guide Yourself Through Recovery 79

Introduction

I am so glad you are reading this book. I know it took courage and determination to get here. You have probably had to self-advocate and self-educate for many years. You might not even have an official diagnosis of obsessive-compulsive disorder (OCD), just a strong intuition that you have it. Whatever the stage of your OCD recovery, I hope this workbook is helpful.

For most of my life, I believed I was just very anxious, so I would never have picked up a book for OCD. Statistically, OCD is diagnosed 14 to 17 years after onset; my diagnosis took 21 years. At the time, I was already a practicing therapist. My master's in counseling gave me only a basic understanding of OCD. I had never even heard of exposure and response prevention (ERP). Eventually, I learned how to heal by reading—just like you are today.

I wrote this book from a place of understanding and compassion. I am an OCD experiencer, a mom of a child with OCD, and an OCD specialist. I have walked this road with hundreds of clients. OCD work is not a place for judgment or cruelty. We all deserve care and kindness.

Simply put, ERP is the best treatment for OCD—and it is also the scariest. But when you begin, you will see that ERP can be a slow, deliberate, and gentle process. You can modify your treatment plan for your unique needs and create supportive structures along the way.

While the word "exposure" may sound harsh, it simply refers to the practice of facing fears through mindful challenges. Despite the term, the effectiveness of ERP is undeniable, with success rates over 80 percent. Here is what some clients have said:

> *"ERP wasn't bad once I got into it. And it worked! In three months, I overcame fears that had hounded me for years."*

> *"I read five books about ERP before I started. I thought it was scary as hell. At first, I was confused. I overexposed myself and panicked—but only once. Then it became a fun puzzle, like an escape room from my OCD."*

> *"I wanted to talk about my OCD and research it. I wanted to learn everything I could about why I was anxious. I wanted to think my way out of OCD. But doing exposures is what made me better."*

I aim to guide you through this process as skillfully as I do with all my clients. In this book, I offer you a gentle, self-compassionate version of ERP—the version I needed when I was most scared. Please note that this workbook is not intended to address severe OCD on its own. If your OCD symptoms are so severe that you unable to work, sleep, or eat, please get medical help in addition to using any self-help resources. Wherever you are in your healing journey, know that you are safe, worthy, and loved. You can heal. You *deserve* to heal.

Before You Begin

Starting this book is your first exposure. An exposure is an act of bravery. You are trusting yourself to do something hard. You are stepping outside your comfort zone to grow and recover. Well done! Here are the nuggets of wisdom I share on day one of ERP treatment with my clients:

Talk therapy can make OCD worse. Many therapists try to treat OCD through talk therapy. Just talking about our worries and our fears can intensify our OCD. OCD specialists use ERP, which is the gold-standard treatment. A few supplemental therapies can help, like acceptance and commitment therapy (ACT), dialectical behavior therapy (DBT), or cognitive behavioral therapy (CBT). However, the backbone and the first line of defense in OCD treatment should be ERP.

OCD is not an anxiety disorder. OCD leads to anxious feelings, but it is a *neurobehavioral* disorder. It is in a completely different diagnostic category than anxiety. It requires a distinct treatment, which is focused not on our feelings but on our behaviors. Anxiety is just a by-product of the cycle of obsessions and compulsions.

We cannot change our thoughts, just our actions. OCD causes intrusive thoughts. In OCD treatment, we do not try to control our thoughts. In fact, we radically accept all thoughts. We focus instead on changing our actions in response to thoughts. When we stop compulsions and confront our fears, the thoughts have less power.

Sometimes OCD attaches to a rational worry. Not all OCD-related worries are outrageous. Sometimes our obsessions center on a rational fear. However, when OCD attaches to anything, real or not, it exaggerates the severity, probability, and consequences of that fear because our threat perception is skewed. Even if the worry makes sense, our response to the worry is outsized.

The "P" in ERP is the most important part. Yes, exposures matter, but they will not make us better unless we *prevent* our compulsions. Response prevention (RP) is often overlooked by those who don't fully grasp how ERP therapy works. Exposures can backfire and make our OCD worse if we immediately follow them with compulsions. Years of living with untreated OCD comes at a cost, but for many of us, it is all we know.

Only start ERP when you feel ready to tolerate the distress of an exposure without trying to solve it. Be sure you fully understand what ERP does and why you are choosing this path. When you are ready to consent with your whole heart to change, that is when you are ready for ERP. Facing your fears is a choice no one can or should force you to make. This path is a personal trade-off: temporary distress for long-lasting peace.

PART ONE

How OCD Responds to ERP

In this part of the book, you will learn about OCD and how well it responds to ERP. These first three chapters serve as a guide for understanding your OCD as well as the discomfort and, yes, the healing that come with this approach. This information will help you prepare for the work ahead in part two. It will ground you in knowledge and self-compassion, setting the stage as you move forward into the process of ERP. You may be excited to get started, but wait until you understand how to do ERP gently and systematically so it can help you be successful.

What to Know About OCD

1

This chapter lays the groundwork for your understanding of OCD. The more we understand OCD, the more we can distance ourselves from the intrusive thoughts. Often, we have had the condition for so long that we struggle to differentiate our personality from our OCD. It's normal to feel resistant at first; many of us initially struggle with labeling our behaviors as part of OCD. Remember to revisit this chapter once you begin the ERP exercises. Learning about OCD is an ongoing process.

A Surprisingly Common Medical Condition

OCD is a cycle in which the brain produces unwanted thoughts, mental images, and urges, and we respond to them to feel better. This response provides temporary relief but reinforces the original fear. Then the cycle begins again. Let's look at each word in the term "obsessive-compulsive disorder" for clarity:

"Obsessive" refers to the repetitive, intrusive thoughts, mental images, and urges.

"Compulsive" refers to the mental and physical actions that soothe the obsession.

"Disorder" refers to the fact that this is a mental disorder that causes distress.

It is estimated that roughly 1 in 40 people have OCD. Most OCD specialists believe that this is a significant underestimation. In many cases, OCD is misdiagnosed as generalized anxiety disorder (GAD). It is often through personal research that people discover that OCD better describes their experience. Unfortunately, it takes between 14 and 17 years from onset of OCD for an adult to get a diagnosis.

Despite this, OCD is a relatively common mental health condition in the United States, affecting millions of people. None of us are alone in this. There is a vibrant online community on Instagram, TikTok, Reddit, and the International OCD Foundation (IOCDF) website for people with OCD. Some members, including me, gather annually at learning and bonding events hosted by the IOCDF.

It is unclear exactly what causes OCD, but there is strong scientific evidence that the tendencies are hereditary. When working with someone who has OCD, I usually ask, "Who else in your family might be experiencing this?" Often, a parent or grandparent has strong indications of OCD, even if undiagnosed. Other contributing factors are differences in brain chemistry, environmental factors such as trauma, personality tendencies, and even certain types of infections that might lead to brain inflammation.

Regardless of OCD's cause, ERP is an effective therapy. In certain cases, ERP may need to be paired with a trauma therapy, such as eye movement desensitization and reprocessing (EMDR), or a medical intervention for brain inflammation. When multiple family members in one household have OCD, family therapy may be needed to disrupt unhealthy patterns.

What All OCD Types Share

OCD usually involves imbalances in neurotransmitters. These are the chemical messengers that allow the brain and the body to communicate. Of particular note are serotonin, glutamate, and gamma-aminobutyric acid (GABA).

- Low serotonin levels are believed to worsen OCD, but the role of this happy chemical in OCD is complex and not fully understood.
- People with OCD tend to have higher levels of glutamate, an excitatory chemical, which encourages the brain to send messages. It is involved in the urge to act on a compulsion.
- People with OCD tend to have lower levels of GABA, an inhibitory chemical that makes us calmer.

I often explain it like this: If your OCD brain were a car, GABA would be the brakes and glutamate would be the gas pedal. Serotonin is doing something important under the hood, but we aren't sure what.

Due to these chemical imbalances, the OCD brain gives us a usually misguided sense that something is wrong and wants us to urgently respond to that feeling of wrongness. It wants us to act on this terrifying feeling to make it better. But when we interact with this feeling of wrongness, we solidify in our minds that what we fear is real. Though self-soothing provides short-term relief, it can increase our fear in the long term.

ERP flips the script. This therapeutic approach encourages us to lean into the fear and not self-soothe. At first, it is incredibly difficult to resist our compulsions, but with time and practice, we strengthen our skills. When we practice ERP, we learn to put the car in park. We start to feel more confident about doing nothing when our OCD really wants us to act. With time, ERP will change our brain by creating new neural pathways.

How Thoughts, Feelings, and Body Sensations Create Confusion in OCD

Before you begin ERP, you must internalize one fundamental idea: Thoughts are not facts. OCD tries to trick us into believing that our thoughts are facts and quite important. OCD can also make us believe that our thoughts have the power to create or cause something out in the world. People without OCD get intrusive thoughts, too, but they can dismiss them as meaningless. With OCD, we often believe that our intrusive thoughts are meaningful and that they can actually be dangerous—but just *our* thoughts, not anyone else's!

Learning to have a healthier relationship with your thoughts is a fundamental part of OCD recovery. If you are trying to control your thoughts, OCD will be able to control *you*. If you allow intrusive thoughts to come and go as they please, without attaching any significance to them, then you are in a much better place to begin ERP.

The Nature of Thoughts

Our incredible thinking abilities set us apart from other species. However, not all thoughts are important, intelligent, or meaningful. Thoughts are electrochemical activity in the brain. They can be an opinion, an idea, a memory, or a spark of imagination. The human brain is trying to understand the world, make connections, and plan for safety.

Thoughts can be conscious or unconscious, and neither can be controlled by willpower. Psychological studies have clearly shown that trying to repress thoughts is ineffective and that thoughts come back stronger when we try to hold them back. That's why the OCD treatment maxim is "What we resist persists."

OCD often causes an excessive occurrence of intrusive thoughts, which are thoughts that are disturbing, repetitive, and unwanted. They can feel like they happen *to us* rather than being produced *by us*. Often, intrusive thoughts increase in frequency due to a change in brain chemistry, including imbalances in the chemical messengers introduced earlier: GABA, serotonin, and glutamate.

Intrusive thoughts also occur more often when we are stressed. In these moments, the amygdala—the fight, flight, freeze part of our brain—becomes overactive. The brain thinks we are in danger, so it scans the world for threats and uses them to generate intrusive thoughts. A couple of common examples include, "I am going to swerve into oncoming traffic," and "Everything is contaminated."

Intrusive thoughts can show up as desires or intentions, or they can pop in as what-if statements. They can be images or words. That said, intrusive thoughts typically reflect our fears rather than our desires.

OCD treatment aims to show us that our intrusive thoughts are not real or true. However, in the face of scary intrusive thoughts, using ERP can feel like a personal trust fall. We cannot truly *feel* that our thoughts are not real or true until we can *act* as if they aren't.

The Meaning of Emotions

Thoughts create emotions. If we are constantly thinking of all the possible ways our loved ones can die, for instance, we are undoubtably going to feel sad. However, these feelings are not facts. These feelings are the creation of our OCD brain, which wants to keep us worried and upset even when something bad is not actually happening. In this way, OCD makes us emotional about events that have not or even will not happen. When we are emotional, we are not evaluating our circumstances in a rational way. These emotional responses help OCD control our actions and make choices from a place of fear.

Please note that I am not discounting our emotions. Each person's emotions are valid to them. The trick, however, is to see an emotion as valid without validating the underlying intrusive thought or worry. While they feel just as deep and painful, your emotions might be based on a complete OCD falsehood.

As an OCD therapist, my approach is different from that of a therapist who specializes in other areas. While emotional connection is often a big part of therapy, with OCD, too much emotional attunement can actually reinforce the condition. So, sometimes the most compassionate approach is for me to be less emotionally attuned. This is true for OCD specialists and for those who care about someone with OCD.

Working with Body Sensations

Just as OCD can create false thoughts and reactive emotions, it can also create bodily sensations. People with germ fears will tell you that they can feel contamination, even when it is on a microbial level. For them, the sensation of clean or dirty is a physical one, not just a mental belief. People with a fear of vomiting, which is commonly referred to by its clinical name emetophobia, constantly feel nauseous. If someone has a fear of having a psychotic break, they can physically experience derealization, lightheadedness, and tinnitus and can even have mild hallucinations.

The most extreme OCD-related bodily sensations I've personally experienced were the symptoms of a real-seeming pregnancy, including pelvic swelling, morning sickness, and the butterfly-like sensation of early fetal movement. My OCD fabricated these symptoms, mimicking my previous pregnancies.

I give these few examples to drive home the point that OCD can create true bodily sensations that are built completely on a false OCD story. While so much mental health guidance urges us to attune to our bodily sensations, OCD therapy helps us learn to not take them so seriously.

How ERP Can Help

With all these contradictory symptoms, you can probably see how talk therapy could cause further confusion about what is real and what isn't. ERP therapy works because it takes you out of thinking loops and encourages concrete action. It challenges you to do the opposite of what your OCD tells you to do.

When you break an OCD rule (i.e., you don't engage in the compulsion), you often have a corrective emotional experience (CEE). This means that life gives you an experience that is different from what you were expecting. The OCD brain wants you to believe that something terrible will happen if you face your fears and don't engage in your compulsions. However, CEEs help you see that this is not necessarily true. As you practice more exposure challenges and resist your compulsions, your confidence grows.

Compassionate ERP means encountering triggers in a safe and measured way. You are never trying to cause yourself overwhelm or panic. Exposures should make you uncomfortable, but tolerably so. Doing ERP slowly will help you have a positive experience that naturally corrects some of your negative beliefs; you start shifting your perspective on triggers and experience less fear.

Common Subtypes of OCD

OCD manifests in infinite ways. After working with hundreds of OCD clients, I still hear about new compulsions and obsessions. In this workbook, you will learn that the particular theme of OCD doesn't really matter. The cycle is essentially the same for all of us. However, it is worth being familiar with the most common subtypes as the content of the exposure challenges will be different. Chances are, you experience a version of at least one of these:

Contamination OCD: You are afraid that you or your home could be contaminated by something dangerous and not just germs—for example, you change clothes at the doorway and have designated inside and outside clothes.

Disgust OCD: You feel a physical repulsion to sounds, textures, and smells, and feel the need to control your environment to reduce this extreme ick—for example, you eat alone to avoid hearing other people chewing.

Existential OCD: You ruminate on the purpose of life and the nature of reality—for example, you have intrusive thoughts like *How do I know if I am who I am supposed to be?*

Harm OCD: You fear that you will harm someone or yourself, accidentally or intentionally—for example, you have a fear of driving off a bridge.

Health OCD: You fear that there is something terribly wrong with your body—for example, you research stroke symptoms because your eye twitched.

Just Right OCD: You need to repeat something until it feels just right—for example, you adjust the volume on the stereo in intervals of five because any other number feels wrong.

Pedophilia OCD: This is the deep-seated fear of being sexually attracted to children—for example, you go out of your way to avoid children because you fear you might molest them. (This is related to harm OCD and sexual orientation OCD.)

Real Event/False Memory OCD: You make an obsessive effort to recollect past events to the point where OCD may implant false memories—for example, you replay the events of the day and become increasingly convinced that you did something dangerous.

Relationship OCD: You fear that you are in the wrong relationship or that you will lose your relationship—for example, you compulsively check a significant other's location to see if they are cheating.

Scrupulosity OCD: You have an intense worry that you are doing something morally or religiously wrong and that you are a bad person—for example, you overapologize for an imagined slight.

Sensorimotor OCD: You are overattentive to or hypervigilant of automatic bodily functions, like breathing, blinking, and swallowing—for example, you fear that you will forget how to breathe or will never be able to stop thinking about breathing.

Sexual Orientation OCD: You worry obsessively that you have a different sexual orientation from the one you present to the world—for example, you have intrusive thoughts like *What if I am not really gay and I am just pretending?*

Symmetry OCD: You feel a need for things to be balanced or exactly fair and equal—for example, you crack your knuckles evenly on both hands.

This is not the only way to categorize OCD subtypes. Some OCD researchers include a category called pure O OCD. Pure O stands for purely obsessional. While compulsions are present, they primarily occur mentally (this can be the case for any subtype). Other researchers put checking OCD into its own category, though most subtypes have compulsions involving checking, repeating, and reassuring.

The Yale-Brown Obsessive Compulsive Scale (YBOCS), which is the best definitive assessment for OCD, solves this dilemma by including *miscellaneous obsessions* and *miscellaneous compulsions* in the categories on its screener. In truth, most categories have significant crossovers, and few people with OCD experience only one subtype. How OCD manifests may also shift and change during one's lifetime. It is common to experience many different presentations of OCD, but they may not always be recognized as such.

Later in this workbook, you will begin building your exposure hierarchy for ERP. I will help you create a treatment approach that is unique to your OCD. However, the underlying principles of ERP do not vary between subtypes of OCD, so most of the activities in this workbook should help.

But My OCD Is Different . . .

OCD stokes fear and skepticism to maintain control of your brain and actions. As you are reading this, you may be experiencing a barrage of intrusive thoughts: *This won't help me. My OCD is different. I won't be able to do exposures.* This is normal. As soon as you begin doing something concrete to get better, your OCD will start acting up and planting doubts.

The truth is: Yes, your OCD is different. And, at the same time, your OCD is very much the same. OCD's individuality is like that of the human face. Our faces are unique enough to use as a secure unlock method on our phones, but the fundamental composition is common in all of us.

Your OCD is a manifestation of your deepest fears, which are unique to you based on your history, culture, and beliefs. OCD is connected to something especially important and essential to you. However, the brain's cyclic response to those fear triggers is what unites us all. The call-and-response nature of obsessions and compulsions transcends any individual version of OCD.

You may also be reading this book thinking, *Actually, I don't think I even have OCD.* Keep in mind that OCD is a doubt and uncertainty disorder. It will sow doubt whenever possible. I am not a fan of excessively labeling mental health conditions and believe a certain amount of skepticism is healthy. However, resistance to the label should not detract from the potential benefit of the solutions offered here.

And, finally, you may feel skeptical of ERP; almost everyone does before they start. But you picked up this book because your cycle of fears and compulsions isn't working for you. Trust in that desire to change, even if you cannot trust in the process quite yet. In chapter 4, I will offer further guidance on how to tailor ERP to your readiness level.

A Typical OCD Experience Before ERP

An important part of OCD work is identifying true OCD cycles and distinguishing them from personality, habit, and preferences. So let's break down what happens in an OCD cycle, moment by moment. Keep in mind that this complex cycle can happen subconsciously and imperceptibly; you might experience it as a pang of fear followed by a frenzy of activity. Understanding your OCD on a granular level will help you structure appropriate exposures later.

An unwanted thought arises.

OCD often starts with an intrusive thought. You might be going about your day pleasantly and then randomly think something like *What if I have cancer?* Sometimes the intrusive thought hits you like a ton of bricks, and sometimes you feel largely unaffected. Remember that everyone has intrusive thoughts, but people with OCD have a much greater tendency to take them seriously.

An unwanted thought can also be a worry triggered by something concrete that you notice. These thoughts, while less random, are usually outsized. In this case, you might notice a mole on your chin that you have had for years and think, *What if that is cancer?*

The mind/body responds.

You may have an immediate physical response to your thought. You are flooded with anxiety, and the thought feels very real. Suddenly, you may be experiencing symptoms you didn't have before the intrusive thought.

Fear is triggered.

When the mind and body respond to the intrusive thought, the feeling of danger is reinforced. The fact that you are anxious might start to give you anxiety. You can become wholly disconnected from the present moment and become too attuned to your own inner process. Without anything happening or changing, you can feel like you are in acute danger. To use the skin cancer example, you don't need to see a perceptible difference in that mole to feel like it is an emergency.

Discomfort arises.

You start to feel uncomfortable moving forward with whatever you were doing and become hyperfocused on the anxiety because you struggle to tolerate any level of fear. The fact that you are anxious suggests to you that you must act quickly.

The self-soothing urge is triggered.

You are now completely in your head about your trigger. You may be overwhelmed with the urge to fix or stop the anxiety. Your brain scans for potential solutions to our fears. Whatever else you were doing seems secondary to solving your problem.

Neutralizing ritual is engaged; that is, you engage in the compulsion.

You turn to your set of go-to behaviors, which you likely have after so many triggering episodes. You might research, check, count, scan, wash, seek reassurance, mentally replay, or, more recently, ask AI for help.

All these behaviors—mental or physical—are forms of neutralization for your anxiety. If you are lucky, you may get a release of dopamine, which creates a positive feeling, from this neutralizing ritual. For example, you might feel some comfort and safety after the AI chatbot tells you that a skin cancer mole has jagged edges but your mole does not.

Relief is temporary.

Unfortunately, this relief doesn't last. The temporary high is followed by a dopamine withdrawal. You get the sense that you have not actually put this issue to bed. You are starting to think about your other moles or future potential moles. Your brain starts scanning for other potential dangers because the relief has quickly given way to another bout of anxiety.

The OCD cycle is reinforced.

Engaging in your compulsions, or neutralizing behaviors, reinforced your fear. You acted on the unwanted thought and therefore made it seem even more real in your mind. Your hypervigilance planted more seeds of doubt.

The comfort you feel when you do a compulsion can be addictive. As soon as it is out of your system, you want more. You want to feel that security and safety, even if for a short moment. Over time, you keep chasing this feeling of peace even though you know it doesn't last.

Another unwanted thought arises.

You will continue to have unwanted thoughts, in part because you reacted. OCD uses whatever it can to get your engagement and attention. The trigger worked. And by treating OCD thoughts and fears as fact, you legitimize them. The line between imagination and reality has gotten blurred because you have treated thoughts as facts and acted on them.

This behavior encourages the OCD to continue to bait you. If you think of OCD as a bully in your head, your reactions to the provocations are what make you a good target. A bully needs attention for the dynamic to thrive.

As you explore compassionate ERP, you will learn that you can interrupt your OCD cycle. It is not pleasant, but neither is the repetitive nature of OCD. Through ERP, you are choosing temporary discomfort. You are openly embracing anxiety because self-soothing your anxiety has gotten you stuck in these cycles.

ERP helps create new neural pathways. You learn to respond differently, and it throws off the entire cycle. While the first few steps in the OCD cycle are inevitable, ERP offers an exit ramp. You cannot control your thoughts or emotions, but you *can* change how you react to them.

The ERP Exit Ramp off the OCD Cycle

Compassionate, Self-Guided ERP

2

This chapter is the nuts and bolts of ERP. Unlike other forms of therapy, ERP requires you to learn the *why* and the *how* of the treatment. When you fully understand the treatment, you may be more apt to be patient and compassionate with yourself. Hopefully, understanding how ERP works will help you stay the course, even when it gets tough. This chapter provides high-level explanations but also sample ERP plans. I personally learn best from examples, so I will provide lots of those!

The Goals of ERP Therapy

Exposure and response prevention (ERP) is a behavioral therapy. In other words, it is not focused on your feelings but on your behaviors. ERP is meant to change how you respond to fear stimuli. The goal is not to form a deep and meaningful connection with a therapist but rather to receive time-limited support that guides you out of maladaptive patterns.

ERP is technically a form of cognitive behavioral therapy (CBT) but contradicts many of the principles of CBT. Unlike CBT, ERP doesn't involve much analysis or discussion. In CBT, you learn to reframe negative thoughts into positive ones. In ERP, you purposefully provoke negative thoughts to practice resisting compulsions. CBT is meant to calm anxiety, whereas ERP (temporarily) provokes it.

The International OCD Foundation (IOCDF) generally discourages self-guided ERP and advises people to work with a specialized clinician. However, accessibility is a major problem in our therapeutic community, and very few people can follow this recommendation. The more common choice is self-guided ERP versus no ERP at all.

I personally believe that self-guided ERP can work well, because in some ways, the technique is relatively simple. The biggest drawback to working without a therapist is the lack of a compassionate accountability partner. I suggest that you pair self-guided ERP with a free support group (available online and in person). If there isn't a support group available to you, consider starting one! Compassionate, self-directed ERP works best when you have caring people cheering you on.

How This Book's ERP Works and Why

This book breaks down ERP into bite-sized pieces. If you feel overwhelmed by the big picture, focus instead on just one piece. OCD brains like to predict the future and catastrophize. Sometimes we struggle to get started with a difficult and complex task because it feels unmanageable. If any part of this journey feels like too much, just back up and redo an earlier section. These steps do not have to be taken in a linear manner (in fact, recovery is not linear at all!). If your brain, like mine, skips around from task to task, then allow yourself that luxury as you start.

Truly, there is no perfect or right way to do ERP. In my experience, most people achieve measurable relief in their symptoms even when they do ERP imperfectly, so long as they stay engaged in the process and don't give up. Because of this, I encourage you to avoid self-criticism and self-blame as you work your way through this process. Even though I am an experienced OCD specialist, I still make mistakes with ERP, especially when I am guiding myself! Embrace imperfection in this process because most mistakes provide insight and still lead to growth.

The supplies for these exercises depend on the nature of your OCD. Mostly, you will need basic office and art supplies, as well as a journal for ERP tracking beyond this workbook or any time you need more space than what's provided. Most of the supplies for your exposures will be whatever you have on hand that triggers your OCD. Occasionally, you may need to bring in a useful prop to support treatment. At my OCD center, I stock up on my ERP props around Halloween: fake blood, amputated arms, pens shaped like needles, realistic giant hornets, and so forth. Exposures can be as silly as they are serious; humor helps when you are taking your power back from OCD.

I will also direct you to the internet for certain exposures. YouTube is particularly useful to introduce fears because of its vast collection of fictional and real triggers. However, many of us also use the internet for compulsions. When I guide you to online exposures, I will also caution you against misuse of this resource.

Let's now look at the steps to your work moving forward.

Build your understanding of your OCD.

The first—and arguably the most crucial—step is to really get to know your OCD. I want you to be able to recognize which behaviors (or thoughts, in the case of pure O OCD) are compulsions and which thoughts are obsessions.

Claim emotional distance from your OCD.

Once you have established self-awareness around your OCD, it is time to practice separating yourself from it. Before you begin work, your OCD might be *ego-syntonic*, which means you largely agree with the obsessive thoughts and compulsive behavior. The goal is to become *ego-dystonic*, which means that you and your OCD are not aligned.

Build internal resources.

You will learn skills for distress tolerance, nervous-system awareness, and emotional regulation. While ERP intends for you to experience anxiety (in fact, it purposefully triggers it), you also do not want to get flooded—that is, experience an overwhelming surge of anxiety and distress. Compassionate ERP means knowing your limits and being able to re-regulate if you are approaching them.

Build external resources.

I will encourage you to connect with the incredible OCD community, both online and in person. I believe we are one of the most tight-knit and internally supportive mental health communities out there. I will also encourage you to build up your existing external resources, mostly the friends and family members who are most excited to see you succeed.

Create a master list of obsessions, compulsions, and intrusive thoughts.

This step will help you organize the fears, behaviors, and thoughts related to your OCD. It can initially be tricky to know what is OCD-related and what isn't, but it is a crucial part of self-guided ERP. This workbook will provide concrete examples and sample master lists from other people with OCD to help you.

Create an exposure hierarchy.

Consider this your ERP to-do list! I will prompt you to get creative and list many ways to challenge your OCD. You will start with easy exposures that help you feel confident in this process and work up to some challenges that have evaded you for years. At the top of the list might be some exposures that feel completely unachievable when you start.

Guide yourself through recovery.

This step requires the most self-compassion. As you move through self-guided ERP, you will need to resist the urge to either withdraw from the process or rush through it. You may pause ERP to attend to your needs or recover from difficult moments, then recommit to the exposures. Sustainable recovery is more important than a fast recovery.

Establish strategies for relapse prevention.

Relapse will happen. It is a completely normal part of recovery. However, you can prepare for how you will handle it when OCD tries to wiggle back into your life. Usually, OCD tries a completely new tactic during relapse. Reading sections of this book that do not specifically pertain to your OCD subtype might help you discern if a new theme takes hold in the future.

Five Sample ERP Exposures Plans

These sample exposure plans are based on the work of real clients. All the clients for whom these exposure hierarchies were created are now in recovery, though there were some bumps along the way. Exposure plans are designed for good enough—not perfect—implementation.

Exposure Plan Instructions

Method: These exposures are to be done one by one and repeated until they are boring. Level up and down as needed. Exposure hierarchies are not meant to be implemented rigidly.

Response Prevention: These exposures are to be done without mental or physical compulsions. If you cannot resist your compulsions, simply go down to an earlier and easier exposure. Keep practicing until you feel mastery.

Rating System: Each exposure includes a standard units of distress (SUDS) rating from 1 to 10, with 1 being mildly annoying, 5 being incredibly uncomfortable, and 10 being panic-attack inducing. Before each exposure, predict your SUDS rating and record it. After completing the exposure, record your actual SUDS rating.

EXAMPLE 1: HARM OCD WITH KNIVES EXPOSURE PLAN

Goal: To be able to use kitchen knives without fear.

		Predicted SUDS	Actual SUDS
Level **1**	Holding a knife for one minute.	3	1
Level **2**	Watching one episode of a knife-forging show.	4	3
Level **3**	Waving a knife around another person.	6	4
Level **4**	Holding a knife for 15 minutes while having a conversation.	6	5
Level **5**	Watching a video about knife accidents.	6	6
Level **6**	Writing a fictitious story about accidentally stabbing someone I love.	6	8
Level **7**	Holding a knife for one hour while doing other tasks.	7	1
Level **8**	Holding a knife up to someone's arm for one minute.	8	8
Level **9**	Role-playing an accidental stabbing with a friend.	8	4
Level **10**	Watching a video about intentional kitchen stabbings.	9	3
Level **11**	Holding a real knife up to my own wrist veins.	10	8
Level **12**	Ripping up a stuffed animal with a knife.	10	4

EXAMPLE 2: FEAR OF VOMITING EXPOSURE PLAN

Goal: To be able to enter public places with ease during norovirus season.

Level		Predicted SUDS	Actual SUDS
Level **1**	Writing and saying the word "vomit."	2	1
Level **2**	Seeing how many synonyms a friend and I can come up with for the word "vomit."	3	1
Level **3**	Writing a fictitious story about vomiting at work.	3	1
Level **4**	Looking at pictures of real vomit online.	5	4
Level **5**	Listening to two minutes of vomit sounds (available on YouTube).	6	6
Level **6**	Watching vomit scenes from mainstream movies.	7	5
Level **7**	Listening to vomit sounds while eating a snack.	8	9
Level **8**	Role-playing vomiting over a toilet with a friend.	9	3
Level **9**	Going to public places that my OCD associates with vomit.	10	5
Level **10**	Listening to vomit sounds in the car before and after going to public places that my OCD associates with vomit.	10	6

EXAMPLE 3: RELATIONSHIP OCD EXPOSURE PLAN

Goal: To be able to say no to my partner without fearing they will be angry with me.

		Predicted SUDS	Actual SUDS
Level **1**	Not calling my partner back immediately.	3	5
Level **2**	Saying no to a favor my partner asks for.	5	7
Level **3**	Not volunteering for a task my partner could do themselves.	5	2
Level **4**	Not matching my partner's enthusiasm about an activity/plan.	5	5
Level **5**	Interrupting a conversation with my partner when I'm busy.	7	7
Level **6**	Going one week without apologizing to my partner.	8	4
Level **7**	Going one week without asking my partner if they are mad at me.	10	4

EXAMPLE 4: FEAR OF DYING OCD EXPOSURE PLAN

Goal: To be able to accept that death is a part of life and reduce the activation around these thoughts.

		Predicted SUDS	Actual SUDS
Level **1**	Writing a general story about death.	5	3
Level **2**	Playing a card game that centers on death.	6	3
Level **3**	Watching a video depiction of a funeral.	6	2
Level **4**	Writing a specific story where a loved one dies.	8	7
Level **5**	Watching a show where a beloved character dies.	8	2
Level **6**	Visiting a cemetery for 10 minutes.	9	7
Level **7**	Drawing my own tombstone.	10	4
Level **8**	Reading the tombstones at a cemetery for one hour.	10	3
Level **9**	Visiting a morgue.	10	9
Level **10**	Writing my own eulogy.	10	8

EXAMPLE 5: FEAR OF DRIVING EXPOSURE PLAN

Goal: To be able to drive again without fear.

Level	Exposure	Predicted SUDS	Actual SUDS
Level **1**	Writing a fictitious story about crashing a car.	3	3
Level **2**	Watching 10 minutes of YouTube videos of slow-moving car accidents.	4	7
Level **3**	Driving in a parking lot with a friend supervising.	5	4
Level **4**	Playing a driving video game and crashing.	6	3
Level **5**	Playing a VR driving game and crashing.	6	2
Level **6**	Driving by myself around the block.	7	3
Level **7**	Writing a fictious story about a dangerous car crash in which I die.	8	7
Level **8**	Driving to work on back roads.	8	8
Level **9**	Watching 10 minutes of YouTube videos of fast-moving car accidents.	9	7
Level **10**	Driving someone else's car around the block.	10	8
Level **11**	Driving on the highway for one exit.	10	9
Level **12**	Driving on the highway for three exits.	10	9
Level **13**	Driving to work on the highway.	10	8

While quite different from one another, every exposure plan is designed to slowly prepare the client's nervous system to fully face their triggers. Notice that the OCD theme doesn't change the general format of the exposure treatment. By the time they arrive at the higher levels of exposure, their brains and bodies experienced far less anxiety than they had predicted.

Through practice and patience, exposure hierarchies like these can help you achieve things that seemed unachievable. Regardless of the theme of your fears, you will likely find that your actual distress rarely lives up to your predicted distress.

Boost Your Ability to Succeed

Unfortunately, ERP usually makes you more anxious before it makes you feel better. When you are first pushing back against the OCD, the OCD will fight back. This is known as an extinction burst and is a common feature of all behavioral treatment plans. I encourage my clients, and now you, to embrace this anxiety as a temporary side effect that shows you that the ERP is working. Thankfully, small but noticeable relief will follow the backlash of anxiety symptoms. When you gain mastery over the easier items on your exposure hierarchy, you will feel encouraged and emboldened for the rest. My goal is to lead you to a few early successes that help you brave later exposures.

Significant, life-changing relief usually comes after about three months of ERP. Compared to other therapeutic interventions, it is quite fast acting. Before becoming an OCD specialist, I was accustomed to having clients on my caseload for multiple years. But with OCD treatment, I can't get too attached because my clients get better before the six-month mark!

Sometimes, the results of ERP are truly remarkable. Here are some of the dramatic transformations I have witnessed: A child with a severe fear of vomiting and performance anxiety won a televised cooking competition;

a young man who hadn't left the house in years went back to college; and a woman who was on medical leave for severe panic attacks reentered the workforce and got promoted! These people prove that ERP has life-changing power.

Factors that improve progress include a strong support network whose members take time to learn about OCD. Your loved ones can help most by offering empathy without enabling your compulsions. Reach out to those closest to you and ask them for the support you need while you are doing self-guided ERP. This can look like positive reinforcement when they see us resist our compulsions, telling us that they see how hard we are fighting against the OCD, and noticing our progress.

Time is an essential resource for success in ERP treatment. Most exposure plans are time-consuming, and it is hard to have more than marginal gains if you cannot devote at least a few hours a week to this treatment.

But the most important factor for success is desire. Do you truly desire healing, and are you willing to endure discomfort to get there? If someone is pushing you to get treatment without a total buy-in, success is far less likely. So, before embarking on this journey, make sure to tap into your intrinsic motivation to get better.

Imagine the Life You Want

I often begin a therapeutic relationship with my clients by asking, "If you had a magic wand, what would your life look like?" While most can imagine a life without financial stressors or interpersonal difficulties, they can't quite picture a life without anxiety. After years of complying with the OCD, they often see it as part of their personality. The same may be true for you.

I encourage you to stop at this point and visualize at least one part of your life being completely OCD-free. When I was in your shoes, I visualized sitting on the balcony with my children, enjoying their company, without having to worry about my numerous illogical safety rituals. I couldn't imagine my whole life as free as it is today, but I could at least picture that one lovely scene.

Set Yourself Up for Success

If you are fully ready to heal with ERP, make the active decision to treat it as a priority for the next few months. Successful ERP is committed ERP. Sporadic ERP is not effective. Follow-through and repetition make all the difference. I recommend you wait to start ERP until you can secure these three factors:

1. **Motivation:** Make sure you are very clear about your *why*. The desire to get better must be yours, not anyone else's.
2. **Time:** ERP is like getting in shape; it is all about time and reps. Daily diligence magnifies your results.
3. **Emotional bandwidth:** Start this process only in the *absence* of a major transition, grief, or compromised health. ERP will drain your emotional resources, so avoid starting from a depleted place.

Be Gentle with Setbacks

Even the most wildly successful ERP treatment involves setbacks. These are great opportunities to gain experience and revise your treatment plan. But, primarily, setbacks are a time to practice self-compassion. Everyone relapses to some degree, both during and after treatment.

ERP is highly successful, but this does not mean it is a one-and-done therapy. You may have to repeat these techniques at various points throughout your life. The more compassionate you can be with yourself, the more likely you will have the confidence to get back on the saddle.

The Role of Medication

For many people, medication can be a helpful adjunct to ERP. The most prescribed medication for OCD is a selective serotonin reuptake inhibitor (SSRI) such as Prozac or Zoloft. If you would like to explore medication, consult a doctor who has experience with OCD. To find specialized care in your area, check out the provider directory on the International OCD Foundation website (see the resources section on page 166).

Important note: If you are in an active state of abuse, the process of ERP is *not* recommended. It is essential to first address your immediate safety. For confidential support, contact the National Domestic Violence Hotline at 1-800-799-7233.

Finding an Experienced OCD Clinician

I encourage you to pair this workbook with the support of an experienced clinician if possible. The IOCDF website includes a list of OCD specialists globally, and there is a growing list of telehealth providers. OCD specialists, however, are in short supply, so you may have difficulty getting an appointment right away. That said, I strongly encourage you to wait for the right person rather than work with a nonspecialist who has openings. Most traditional talk therapists lack OCD training, and talk therapy can worsen OCD.

You do not need to like your OCD clinician for them to be a good fit. Remember, this is a short-term intervention, focused on results, not emotions. The most matter-of-fact therapists often get the best results when it comes to ERP. You should feel safe in their presence, but you do not have to have a strong emotional bond with your therapist to make progress.

However, if your OCD therapist wants to move quickly and lacks compassion, look elsewhere. A small minority of OCD clinicians believe in flooding techniques, purposefully overwhelming the nervous system with the hardest version of the fear, which can cause a long-lasting aversion to ERP and usually leads to treatment dropout. An effective OCD therapist will go step-by-step and always lay the groundwork for a difficult exposure.

Readiness Checkpoint

Answer true or false to the following eight statements. If you answer true for all or at least most of them, you are ready for the next chapter.

1. I believe that my OCD is lying to me to gain control over my life.
2. I accept that I cannot control my thoughts and feelings.
3. I am willing to face my anxiety without engaging in a compulsion.
4. I understand that OCD gives me temporary, false comfort that reinforces my fears.
5. I believe that ERP is the gold-standard treatment for OCD.
6. I choose to make time to do daily exposures.
7. I am determined to get better, even if that temporarily makes me more anxious.
8. I have the emotional resources to cope with this process.

If you do not feel ready for the next chapter, do not despair. You can restart this book from the beginning, join an OCD support group, or read a memoir about OCD recovery, such as *Rewind, Replay, Repeat* by Jeff Bell. ERP is far more successful when you are fully invested in the process. I am excited for you to succeed in recovery, but I do not want you to feel pressure to do so right now.

Skills to Build Your Capacity to Change

3

This chapter teaches a handful of skills to improve your ERP success. When it comes to mental health techniques, think of them like throwing spaghetti at the wall to see what sticks. Do not get disheartened if a certain technique doesn't stick for you. Everyone is different. I need easy-to-remember, quick techniques because my brain often goes blank when I am anxious and I have only a few minutes to spare between therapy sessions. Your preferred techniques might be more complex or slower. Prioritize techniques that resonate with you and discard any that don't.

Skills That Support OCD Recovery

Skill building is critical for successful ERP. While it is ideal to have a baseline of competency with these five categories of skills before starting ERP, the truth is that most people don't. That's because OCD erodes our ability to regulate emotions, accept and disengage from thoughts, and be kind to ourselves. Consider these skills to be part of a readiness wish list but also something to develop on an ongoing basis throughout the ERP process. By the way, anyone can benefit from these skills because they help us face life's inevitable challenges with more resilience.

Emotional Distancing

This skill helps you to be less reactive to your emotions. Emotional distancing doesn't mean dismissing emotions. Rather, it is about compassionately acknowledging emotions without wallowing in them. This skill will also support you in getting yourself grounded again if you have been overexposed. Emotional flooding from exposures can be a side effect of self-guided (and even therapist-guided) ERP, so be sure you have solid skills to re-regulate yourself.

Cognitive Defusion

This skill helps you to be less reactive to your thoughts. You can notice thoughts, and even sometimes label them as OCD, without needing to spiral deeper. Cognitive defusion helps you disengage from rumination cycles.

Distress Tolerance

This skill is about learning to sit with discomfort. The more skilled you are at distress tolerance, the more successful you will be at ERP. ERP will teach you how to experience distress without any self-soothing behaviors.

Self-Compassion Skills

Self-compassion does not mean avoidance of exposures. Rather, it means pushing yourself to heal with the kindness you would afford a friend. Unfortunately, many people do not naturally practice self-compassion, so it is a skill that often needs to be honed for successful ERP.

How to Approach Practicing These Skills

Ideally, you would have the time and space to practice the skills in this chapter before embarking on ERP. Perhaps spend a week or two applying these skills in your everyday life. A skill can only truly be learned through repetition and success.

I would love for you to feel confident with your toolbox of skills before moving on to more triggering chapters. My hope for your ERP experience is that it will be an empowering journey from day one. However, I don't want you to get stuck here, waiting for the just right moment to begin ERP. The OCD brain sometimes tells us that we are not ready for hard things. OCD sometimes wants us to overprepare before launching into something new.

Think of this chapter like the dugout in a baseball game. You leave and come back. The skills in this chapter can become a place of safety and recovery. You can and should come back to these skills throughout the ERP process. Most of these skills are widely applicable beyond ERP. Any additional time you spend practicing them will be an investment in your future mental health.

Practice Delaying Compulsions Now

You can prepare for ERP by practicing delaying compulsions. A single obsession is like a persistent itch, and a compulsion is a scratch. Resisting the urge to scratch, even if for just one minute, helps build the neural pathways of self-control. I suggest you practice delaying small compulsions at first and compulsions that are related to your less-activated obsessions.

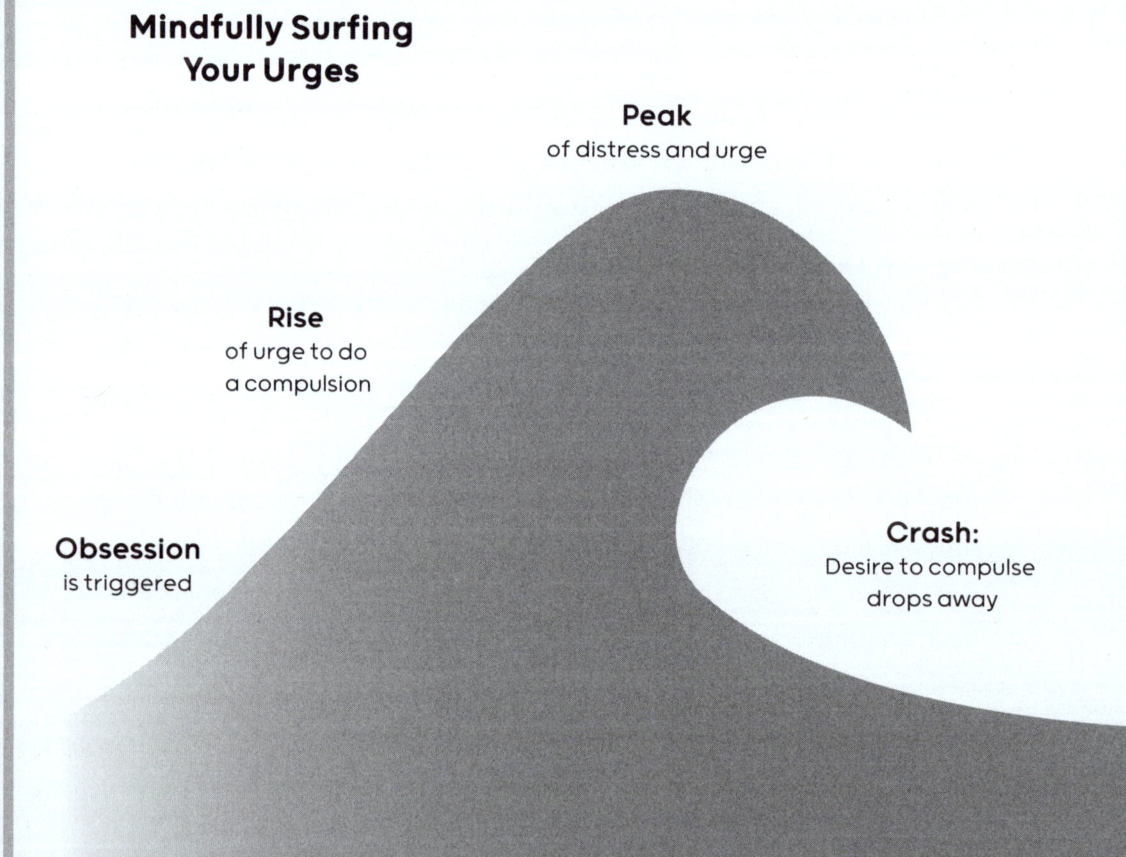

You can also practice by setting up a triggering situation for your OCD. For example, if you have perfectionism or just right OCD, you can leave one kitchen cabinet ajar for the afternoon and keep walking past it, resisting the urge to close it.

Even just delaying a compulsion for a few seconds will plant a seed that leads to increased distress tolerance down the road. Every time you push back against a compulsion, you are undermining the OCD's control and creating a small disruption in the cycle of negative reinforcement. These small moments add up and can make a measurable difference.

I suggest you develop a short visualization practice to substitute for rumination or other go-to mental compulsions. My favorite is to imagine a surfer riding a wave. The obsession is the start of the wave, the compulsive urge is the rise, and the urge to do a compulsion is the peak before it eventually drops off into froth. Neuroscientific research indicates that the urge to do a compulsion follows this wave pattern. Delaying a compulsion for just 20 minutes can start to reshape your neural pathways.

Strong urge becomes a
gentle froth

Emotional Distancing Skills

Developing your emotional distancing skills with practice should help you move through exposures with less emotional activation. Similarly, when your OCD is triggered outside of ERP, you will feel less fused with your emotions.

PRACTICE ACTIVITY

Self-Distancing Visualization

This meditative visualization helps you intentionally depersonalize when you start to become emotionally flooded.

1. Anchor yourself physically to the ground. I like to lie on the floor, but you can also sit on the ground or in a chair with your feet on the floor. You can also visualize yourself connecting with the ground. The idea is to sense that you are supported.

2. Once you are settled into this position, breathe naturally and pay attention to the parts of your body that are solidly held by the ground. All the while, allow the emotions to rise inside you.

3. Whatever emotional expression is needed, let it happen-for example, cry, yell, groan . . . And as you do, accept these unpleasant emotions.

4. After a few minutes, come back to your breath. Imagine you are observing yourself in this grounded position.

5. Now imagine that you are watching yourself from farther away. Pan out and see if you can picture the rest of the room in your mind's eye. Keep zooming up and out until your image of yourself disappears. Try to visualize the green earth and the community that surrounds you.

6. Allow yourself to float in this visualization for a few moments before returning to your body.

   TIP: For those with existential OCD, this visualization may trigger feelings of derealization or depersonalization, making this more of an exposure exercise than an emotional regulation technique. In this case, choose another approach until you have conquered your fear of dissociation.

PRACTICE ACTIVITY

The Time-Warp Technique

In this grounding exercise, you zoom forward or backward to reframe the emotional charge of an experience.

1. Find a comfortable spot in your home. Settle into a restful position, perhaps with a heavy blanket. Close your eyes.

2. Remember a comforting scene from your past or imagine a calm moment in your future. Orient yourself to this scene, trying to imagine and identify details that surround you.

3. Now, from this vantage point of a scene in the present, remember your emotional trigger. Observe it from this temporal distance. Consider it from a new lens.

4. Remain here for a few moments or minutes before getting up and moving on with your day.

   TIP: Visualizations in general can be tricky when we are also dealing with a barrage of intrusive thoughts and a brain that wants to ruminate. The biggest predictor of success with visualizations is consistent practice. If your mind wanders, simply return to the visualization and try again.

PRACTICE ACTIVITY

Lose It, Then Move It

In this exercise, you practice sparking an uncomfortable emotion and using high-intensity movement to dissipate the charge.

1. On your phone, prep one photo, post, or news article that brings up unwanted emotions and one song that energizes you.
2. Pull up the photo/post/article first and purposefully tap into your emotionality. Stay with this emotion for at least 30 seconds or until you are feeling it in your body.
3. Now press play on the song. For the length of the music (three or four minutes is ideal), dance, do jumping jacks, run in place, or perform any sort of high-intensity movement your body allows.
4. When the song ends, take a moment to observe what you are feeling and sensing. Most likely, the emotional response has been replaced by physical exhaustion.
5. If you feel up to it: Repeat!

   TIP: This exercise may need to be adapted for different physical abilities. If you cannot access intense movement, I suggest a deep stretch or a three-minute self-massage during the song.

Cognitive Defusion Skills

Cognitive defusion skills help you avoid taking your thoughts too seriously. With OCD, it is easy to get caught up in intrusive thoughts instead of letting them pass. Cognitive defusion encourages noticing, labeling, and even thanking the thoughts, without ruminating on them. It does not stop the thoughts but makes them less sticky.

When you practice these skills regularly, you will be more able to see thoughts as temporary events of the mind. While you cannot stop intrusive thoughts from entering your mind, you can reclaim your agency around how you interact with them.

PRACTICE ACTIVITY

Rocks by a Stream

This exercise involves taking a deliberate walk along a stream or river to solidify a metaphor that will help you practice letting go of your thoughts. If you do not live near a stream or river, you can do this as a visualization instead.

1. Find a quiet path near a river or stream. Set out on this walk with the intention of having a physical experience of this mindfulness technique.
2. Walk along the path and simply observe the water for a few minutes. These are the events of your life flowing by.
3. Now stop and pick up every rock you see. Examine each rock and then put it into your pocket.
4. When you are starting to feel bored and weighed down, imagine that each rock is a thought. You have picked up every thought, examined it, and held on to it. This represents rumination. The walk alongside the stream has now become unpleasant.
5. Next, dump out the rocks and restart the walk.
6. This time, you are committing to observe the rocks (and the water) but not stopping to pick them up.
7. Choose one rock that looks unique among the masses. You may pick this one up and bring it home.

8. Keep this rock on your nightstand or desk. It is a reminder that you have hundreds of thoughts, like rocks along a stream. Not every thought is worth examining or treasuring. Very few are special or valuable.

9. Remember this scene when you are inundated with intrusive thoughts. Rocks are all around, but you need not pick them up. Keep moving forward.

   TIP: If you cannot go for a walk and would like help with your visualization, you can watch a video on YouTube taken in the first-person perspective of walking alongside a river. However, if you use the internet for compulsions, avoid misusing this resource.

Thoughts and the Stream of Life

PRACTICE ACTIVITY

Burning-Paper Ritual

In this activity, you write down intrusive thoughts on small pieces of paper and observe them slowly burn away. Your intrusive thoughts do not serve you. By burning them, you are signifying that you are not going to cling to your thoughts. You see that they are temporary.

1. Prepare 1 to 10 small sheets of paper.
2. Write down your most common intrusive thoughts, one thought per sheet.
3. In a safe space, light a small fire in a pot, bowl, firepit, or fireplace.
4. Hold one of the sheets of paper with your intrusive thought and intentionally bring this thought to your mind. Let any emotions come in as you hold on to the thought.
5. Now, with an intention of letting go, drop the thought into the fire.
6. Watch the words of the thought burn and imagine that the smoke rising is taking the thought away.
7. Feel into any emotional response resulting from this ritual. Pause at this moment to really notice your experience.
8. Repeat with each thought until you have burned all the slips of paper.

   TIP: For some people with OCD, fire can be a signifier of potential harm and trigger deep-seated fears. If this would be an exposure for you, wait until you have taken the emotional charge out of fire before trying this ritual.

PRACTICE ACTIVITY

Third-Person Narrative

Writing about your OCD fears in the third person helps separate you from your thoughts. Instead of journaling from your own perspective, you will attribute your fears and beliefs to someone else (fictional or real). Externalizing your imagined fears this way helps you rewrite your own internal stories.

1. Choose one what-if story that your OCD tells when it is triggered–for example, "What if I snap and have a nervous breakdown?"
2. Create a hero or villain to be the main character of your story–for example, "Melissa is a diligent and capable mom . . ."
3. Write at least two paragraphs, using descriptive language–for example, "One day, Melissa snapped! She ripped her baby from the crib and carried him angrily toward the steep staircase." Humor and drama help punctuate that OCD is fiction, not fact, so add lots of drama and humor.
4. Conclude your story with a description of the worst-case scenario.
5. Record yourself reading your narrative as if you are telling a scary campfire story.
6. Listen to your recording a few times. With every repetition, the story will probably go from scary to goofy, and finally, to boring.

TIP: This exercise might feel silly in comparison to the gravity of your OCD. I was a harm OCD postpartum experiencer; few things were a laughing matter for me, especially not infanticide. But I made my sweet mom friend Melissa the protagonist of my story because it helped expose the absurdity of my fears. Quality OCD treatment usually contains an element of the theatrical.

Distress Tolerance Skills

Distress tolerance skills help you expand your ability to cope with psychological pain. It is especially important for the response prevention part of ERP because distress tolerance allows you to sit with the discomfort of an exposure without performing a compulsion.

After practicing these skills, you will be less quick to use compulsions to self-soothe. You will be able to pivot away from maladaptive (unhealthy) behaviors. Instead, you will have a toolbox of healthy coping strategies that include mindfulness, distraction, self-soothing, and radical acceptance.

PRACTICE ACTIVITY

Animal-Based Mindfulness

This activity invites you to focus on an animal that is receptive to your attention as a means of centering on the here and now. As you mindfully attend to your pet or to an animal at a shelter or petting zoo, you progressively ground yourself and calm your nervous system. Many animals are receptive to this type of mindful connection.

1. Meet the animal at their level, and spend a few minutes settling into what they might want or need from you.
2. Draw your focus back into a mindfulness practice by quietly observing the animal. What details do you notice about the animal? See if you can spot a unique feature.
3. If the animal is touch-friendly, focus on how they feel on your fingertips. Notice where they are softer and where they are coarse.
4. Allow yourself to drop fully into the here and now alongside this creature. Intentionally use your five senses to be completely present in this moment with this animal.
5. End this mindfulness practice with an expression of gratitude to this creature and the peaceful moment you have experienced with their support.

   TIP: I believe this exercise can be even more impactful for someone who doesn't normally spend time with a pet due to the novelty of the experience. When I worked at a Shanghai-based orphanage, I used slow exposure to help the children get comfortable with a therapy dog, especially since many had never interacted with a pet. However, not everyone feels a connection with animals even after slow exposure, so if you prefer, use a stuffed animal for this exercise.

PRACTICE ACTIVITY

The Cold-Plunge Technique

This strategy for muscle recovery and circulation has become wildly popular in recent years, but few know that cold-water immersion also has tremendous mental health benefits. Cold-plunge rituals are not just a new fad; they have been part of many cultures for centuries. For ERP, cold plunges can be an effective nervous system reset after a difficult exposure.

1. Fill your bathtub with cold water and add ice and/or frozen water bottles to lower the temperature. If you don't have access to a bathtub, then you can fill a large bowl or pot with water and ice.
2. Immerse your body (or your face, if using the large bowl) in the cold water. The cold water will initially shock your system. You will feel your heart rate go up, and you may feel stressed.
3. Within moments, your body will activate the parasympathetic nervous system, decreasing your heart rate and blood pressure. You will experience a feeling of calm.
4. Stay in for 30 seconds or up to 2 minutes. As you acclimate to this activity, you can gradually increase the time in subsequent plunges.
5. When you leave the water, you'll notice an elevated mood. This activity releases dopamine, endorphins, norepinephrine, and other neurotransmitters that improve emotional regulation and reduce stress.

   TIP: The effects of cold plunges can vary from person to person. This activity is not safe for everyone, especially in longer durations. Avoid cold plunges if you have heart problems or Raynaud's phenomenon. When in doubt, consult a doctor.

PRACTICE ACTIVITY

Self-Care Menu

In the exercise, you will create a menu of various self-care activities to turn to when you need to rebalance emotionally. A menu makes it easier to remember how many great options you have when you feel overwhelmed. Use this blank menu to brainstorm ideas and then grab paper and art supplies to create something unique and personal. I like to approach this activity with an artistic flourish, but a simple list can work as well.

1. In the blank menu provided, first list the appetizers. These are 5- or 10-minute self-care activities, such as a walk around the block, a self-massage, or a short guided meditation. In addition to being quick, these self-care activities should be easy and low friction.

2. Next, list at least five options for the main course section of your menu. These items are longer activities, such as hikes, warm baths, bike rides, concerts, or favorite games.

3. Now pick some desserts that include more indulgent and less frequent self-care options. Perhaps desserts will include shopping at a favorite store, dinner out with a friend, or a pedicure.

4. Display your creation or a printout of a photo of the next page and put it in a prominent place in your home where you can refer to it when you are feeling overwhelmed.

   TIP: I encourage you to invest your time and creativity in creating a beautiful menu that is easy to reference. These self-care activities may seem obvious, but when we are tired or overwhelmed, we often default to scrolling or streaming. While these passive activities can also be on your self-care menu, you will be choosing them intentionally.

MY SELF-CARE MENU

APPETIZERS

MAIN COURSE

DESSERT

Self-Compassion Skills

Self-compassion skills are the ability to treat yourself with the same kindness you show others. Self-compassion includes self-love, self-forgiveness, and self-patience. In ERP, self-compassion means you are setting an intention to support yourself through exposures instead of pushing yourself mercilessly.

Practicing these skills will help you be gentle with yourself. With self-compassion, you can accept the challenge of ERP without losing sight of your emotional needs. You must hold your humanity front and center during this healing journey. Self-compassion skills will allow you to pace yourself through the rest of this book and have patience for the inevitable hiccups along the way.

PRACTICE ACTIVITY

Letter to Your Future Self

In this exercise, you will write a classic letter to your future self, who is moving through ERP. You will help your future self celebrate progress and also have patience for mistakes. If possible, use a special pen and a piece of beautiful stationery for this activity.

1. Picture yourself doing an exposure. Try to connect to the emotions you may be feeling and the fears you may be experiencing.
2. Address the letter to yourself, and begin with an uplifting affirmation, something you would love to hear from someone else.
3. Write an encouraging letter, acknowledging that mistakes and detours will be part of ERP work. Before ending, acknowledge the bravery it took to embark on ERP.
4. Seal this letter in an envelope, addressed to yourself.
5. Slip the envelope into the second half of this workbook. It will be there when you most need it.

TIP: If this letter feels strange or hard to write, you are not alone. Many people have difficulty speaking lovingly to themselves. It might even feel arrogant or conceited to do so. The truth is, humans are wired for self-love, but your perspective may be skewed by years of negative self-talk. The only way to rewire these neural pathways is to practice being kind to yourself. The more often you embrace positive self-talk, the more natural it will feel.

Here is a sample letter:

Dear Natalia,

Your determination amazes me. Every time I think you are stuck, you find a way forward.

I am also so proud of your commitment to ERP. I know you were scared before you started this. It must have taken so much courage to get where you are, doing these exposures.

I am writing from before you began. You were struggling because you thought it would be too hard for you. Now you know that the OCD was lying to you. You are stronger than the OCD. You are strong enough to do great things.

But I know you are facing setbacks. This is a normal part of ERP. In fact, it is a necessary part of ERP. You need to make mistakes to learn more about what is limiting you.

Don't forget to have compassion for yourself when you fall. Give yourself affirmations. Give yourself patience.

When you fall, fall forward. Know that you are worthy, even in your messiest moments.

Love,

Natalia

PRACTICE ACTIVITY

The Self-Compassion Home Screen

In this exercise, you will write or find a self-compassion mantra to save on the home screen of your phone. The mantra is a short phrase you can repeat to yourself that gives you comfort and strength. Your mantra may reflect your values and the direction you wish to go with your healing.

1. Visualize yourself doing a hard exposure. Feel into the emotions that are arising in your body just by imagining this fear-inducing experience.
2. Now try to imagine what you most would want to hear in this moment. What short phrase would give you comfort and strength? Here are a few examples of self-compassion mantras:
    - *I am enough.*
    - *I deserve love and patience.*
    - *This is hard. I am doing my best.*
    - *May I give myself the compassion that I need.*
3. On a design app like Canva, create an image with this phrase. Give it a calming aesthetic that you can appreciate. Alternatively, you can use paper and markers to create the image and take a photo of it.
4. Save this image to your photo library on your phone and set it as your home screen wallpaper, where you will see it and repeat it as often as you look at your phone.

    TIP: For some people with OCD, a repetitive phrase can become a mental compulsion. If you feel you ***have*** to say your mantra to neutralize an intrusive thought or to move forward, switch to a new mantra or choose a different form of self-compassion.

PRACTICE ACTIVITY

Self-Compassionate Body Scan

In this body scan, you will send love and attention to areas of your body one at a time. At each juncture, you will express gratitude toward that area of your body, helping to discharge accumulated tension associated with your OCD.

1. Start by lying down on a comfortable surface. If this position makes you too sleepy, switch to a sitting posture.
2. Take a moment to celebrate the fact that you are beginning this practice. It is an act of self-love to take this time and make this effort.
3. Start by simply becoming aware of any physical sensations throughout your body. Some parts might be sore; others might be itchy or twitching. Acknowledge the sensations without judgment.
4. Focus your attention to your breath. Find a comfortable but slow, relaxing rhythm. Visualize the oxygen reaching every part of your body and nourishing you.
5. Now gently move your awareness from your breath to the top of your head. Try to send warmth and sensation to your forehead, ears, and cheeks. Squeeze and release the muscles in your face and then neck.
6. Withdraw attention from your head and neck, and gently move down to your shoulders and chest. Focus on these parts of your body in your mind's eye. Notice and release any sensations that come up. Move this process all the way down your body, until you reach the tips of your toes.

7. Throughout this scan, imagine sending compassion to each part of your body. Thank your strong and resilient body for all the work it does.

8. End by returning to your breath. Feel your whole body rising and expanding with each inhalation.

9. Thank yourself for taking the time to nourish yourself in this way. Notice how you feel after this act of self-love.

TIP: Your body has an inherent wisdom, but sometimes OCD creates bodily sensations to inspire fear. If you have somatic presentations of OCD (in other words, the OCD causes your body to physically react), doing the body scan might highlight your fears. For example, you might feel like your heart is not beating right or your old injury is acting up. Simply allow for these sensations like any other. Do not judge, do not solve, and do not analyze. Just let them be. These sensations will pass like any other.

Readiness Checkpoint

You are ready to move forward when you can practice self-compassion, self-care, and patience. ERP will spark intrusive thoughts and activate unpleasant emotions. If you can ground yourself in emotional and physical safety when this happens, you have prepared yourself sufficiently to keep going. You can revisit the exercises in this chapter anytime during your healing process, as needed.

Answer true or false to the following eight statements. If you answer true for all or at least most of them, you are ready for the next chapter.

1. I can tolerate low-level distress and discomfort related to my OCD triggers.
2. I feel that I can offer myself compassion during moments of activation.
3. I am willing to embrace uncertainty, even if it gives me anxiety to do so.
4. I am committed to allowing emotions to come and go without trying to fix or stop them.
5. I understand that *intrusive* thoughts are not *my* thoughts, and that I do not need to analyze them.
6. I am willing to be courageous during the ERP process and will always find my way back to self-kindness.

7. I do not expect a linear, perfect journey in my OCD healing.
8. If I am flooded, I will return to the exercises in this chapter to re-ground and fortify myself.

If you don't feel ready to move on to part two, you are not alone! Many people struggle to accept the discomfort of purposefully activating fears and resisting compulsions. You may need to spend more time building your distress tolerance. Consider connecting with other OCD experiencers on online forums to learn more about their recovery efforts. The community of people with OCD is very connected and generally quite positive. Many organizations, such as the IOCDF, sponsor events globally and virtually to help motivate those who are earlier in the healing process.

PART TWO

Guide Yourself Through Recovery

Now that you have practiced the skills that support OCD recovery and feel ready to make changes, it is time to begin ERP. Your OCD may try to convince you that you need to prepare more and delay getting started. It may try to convince you that there is a just right moment to begin ERP. There is not. Even with a massive amount of preparation, ERP can still feel like a trust fall. Congratulate yourself for making it this far. Celebrate yourself for moving forward. Do not forget to be self-compassionate; turning the page to this part of the book is an exposure in and of itself. Let's begin.

Your Customized ERP Approach

4

This chapter helps you dissect your OCD so that you can create a highly personalized treatment plan. This process requires you to be detail oriented: *Where and how do you do your compulsions? What exactly are the intrusive thoughts saying? What are the specific situations you are avoiding?* I want you to feel like an OCD detective—nonjudgmental, just curious and observant. As you build out your map of your personal experience of OCD, your customized plan will start taking shape.

Recognize Your OCD Symptoms and Cycles

To start, you need to create a clear road map of your OCD. Because most people with OCD have multiple themes (which can also overlap), categorizing your OCD is not all that useful beyond learning about the condition. In fact, themes become cumbersome during ERP. In ERP, we structure exposures by difficulty, starting with the easiest exposures and building from there.

Instead of categorizing, I find value in helping my clients create a master list of their OCD as obsessions, compulsions, intrusive thoughts, and fear cycles. I call this our O/C/I/F doc, and we refer to it constantly throughout treatment. For my clients, this is the backbone of treatment, even more so than the exposure hierarchy, which you will learn more about soon.

You will find examples of obsessions, compulsions, intrusive thoughts, and fear cycles from the "Sample O/C/I/F Doc Entries" (see page 118) of a few of my courageous clients who believe in paying it forward. You may reference these examples while you create your own O/C/I/F doc, but avoid letting your OCD use them to compare and minimize your experience. Remember, OCD says, "My OCD is different and that treatment won't work for me." Yes, everyone's OCD is different. However, everyone's OCD follows the same basic pattern of call and response, obsession and compulsion. All forms of OCD can respond to ERP treatment.

Here is a quick reminder:

Obsessions: what we fear

Compulsions: what we do when we are afraid

Intrusive Thoughts: unwanted fear thoughts, usually in the form of "What if?"

Fear Cycles: the path by which intrusive thoughts, obsessions, and compulsions fit together and mutually reinforce each other

I find that, at first, most people can't quite differentiate between these four categories. The important part is to get everything on the page, rather than perfectly organized into categories. Once you have more experience doing ERP, the differences will become more pronounced. It is okay if you cannot put your finger on the fear cycles at this point. Again, all this will become clearer as you practice doing exposures and resisting your compulsions.

Here are some questions to help jog your memory as you develop your O/C/I/F doc:

When your mind wanders, where does it go?

How do you react to conflict?

When you lie awake worrying, what do you think about?

When you hear a siren or a crash, what does your brain tell you has happened?

What phrases do you hear yourself say all the time?

What do you do when you feel out of control?

What do you avoid out of anxiety?

What are the things you feel like you need to do every day to prevent something bad from happening?

Does your brain make up a story if you missed a call during the night?

If you don't hear from a loved one in a while, what is your worry?

What are the themes of your nightmares?

How do you cope with uncertainty?

How do you react to change?

What possibility do you most dread?

Not all your answers to these questions will be part of your OCD, but some will. What distinguishes OCD from anxiety disorders is the call-and-response cycle. If you can have a worry and not interact with it further, that is not an OCD cycle. You can dread something without it having OCD–especially if you don't avoid it!

Let me share an example of how the question "When you hear a siren or a crash, what does your brain tell you has happened?" reveals my personal symptoms of OCD:

Obsession: fear of harm to my children

Compulsion: rumination, checking, hypervigilance

Intrusive Thought: *My child is in danger.*

Fear Cycle: I hear a siren, have an intrusive thought that my child is in danger, feel anxious, check their locations on my phone, and then temporarily feel better when I see they are not in an ambulance. The next time I hear a siren, I repeat the cycle because I have reinforced my fear.

Your Personal O/C/I/F Doc

Begin drafting your O/C/I/F doc here. This is only a draft. You can continue to add to and organize it as you proceed through this chapter and workbook. Later, you can make a more formal, categorized version in your journal. See "Sample O/C/I/F Doc Entries" on page 118 for real-life examples in each category.

Self-Monitor Your OCD Symptoms

Once you have created a draft of your O/C/I/F doc, the next step is to practice self-monitoring your symptoms. People with OCD tend to underestimate how much of our day is influenced by the condition. For many, OCD has become second nature and sometimes even blends into what we consider our personality, habits, or quirks.

Becoming aware of the time and effort you spend on OCD cycles *before* you begin ERP will help you justify the energy investment in this treatment. As you self-monitor, you may notice far more compulsions than you originally listed on your O/C/I/F doc.

Many people only begin monitoring their symptoms once they are already doing exposures, which means they don't have a clear account of the OCD *before* treatment. I find this step to be especially valuable for motivation later in ERP. You can look back at your pretreatment symptoms and appreciate the improvement. Use the "Fear and Response Diary" on page 116 to monitor your OCD behaviors and cycles.

Identify Other Triggering Factors

OCD tends to ebb and flow. Certain situations, people, environments, and even news cycles can trigger an episode or series of episodes. For females, the hormonal changes of the luteal phase (one week before period starts) can be a significant trigger.

Answer these questions to identify other factors that may contribute to an uptick in OCD:

What time of day do you feel your OCD is most active?

___

Does your OCD get easier or harder to deal with when you travel?

___

Which friends and family members tend to activate your fear cycles?

___

Do you do fewer or more compulsions when at home?

___

Does your OCD have any seasonal changes?

___

Do you have more OCD tendencies when you have access to your phone?

___

Is your OCD triggered at work?

___

Is your OCD more pronounced when you are busy or relaxing?

___

Do any chronic health concerns worsen your OCD? If so, which ones?

___

___

When you identify other factors at play, you can build more flexibility into your ERP plan. For example, if my client with an autoimmune disorder comes into a session with painful inflammation, we may choose to repeat successful exposures rather than moving up the exposure hierarchy. Not every day is going to be a great day for ERP practice. When you know that other triggering factors that make OCD more challenging are present, you can practice more self-compassion.

Create Your Exposure Hierarchy

While "exposure hierarchy" is a clinical term, this step is really about creating a wish list of challenging activities. In creating this hierarchy, you might consider calling it exposure goals or exposure challenges. A few of my clients have even created colorful names like "F-it bucket list" or "screw-with-the-OCD list." Here are the steps to create your own exposure hierarchy:

1. Answer these questions in any order you wish:

   What have I stopped doing because of my OCD?

   ____

   ____

   ____

   ____

   ____

   ____

What do I see other people doing who don't have OCD?

How could I break the OCD rules (not give in to the compulsion)?

What would be a small step toward facing my OCD fear?

What places do I avoid because of my OCD?

2. Rewrite your answers as tasks on a wish list. For example, if you have stopped traveling internationally because of your OCD, you might write, "Vacation with my partner in Cancun, Mexico."

3. Take each bigger task on your wish list and create three to four smaller challenges that would build up to this task. For example, "Research flights on Expedia," "Visit the international terminal at my airport," or "Have a vacation-planning conversation with my partner."

4. Go back to steps two and three, and add extra items to the list that feel exciting and motivating. You want your challenges to give you a feeling of inspiration, not just dread. The idea is to have many options to choose from as you develop your exposure plans. (See pages 39-43 for examples.)

5. Once you have at least 30 to 40 items on your list, rate each task using the standard units of distress (SUDS) rating from 1 to 10, with 1 being the least anxiety-provoking and 10 being the most anxiety-provoking. Here is an example of the scale:

1	Mildly annoying	**6**	Panic-provoking
2	Annoying	**7**	Significantly panic-provoking
3	Uncomfortable	**8**	Terrifying
4	Anxiety-provoking	**9**	Seemingly impossible level of panic
5	Significantly anxiety-provoking	**10**	Can't even imagine being able to do this

You can use this scale as is or have a little fun with it by changing the descriptions. It only needs to make sense to you.

6. After rating each task, reorder your list from easiest to hardest on the next page.

7. If you rated many of your challenges as 7s, 8s, 9s, and 10s, balance out your tasks by adding easier exposures and imaginary exposures. For example, "Watching a YouTube video from the inside of an international flight" or "Writing a fear story about traveling to Mexico."

This hierarchy is potentially the most challenging step to accomplish without the support of a therapist. When you are still fused with your OCD, it is difficult to imagine steps outside your current system. At this stage of healing, parts of your OCD may feel logical and valuable. If you have a nonjudgmental friend or family member, consider bringing them in for this step for a grounding outside perspective. Sometimes we need another person to do *reality testing*, which is when we anchor ourselves back to the here and now by relying on someone else's thoughts and nervous system.

Also, it is important to note that most exposure hierarchies include items you may never actually do. I rarely reach the 10s with my clients. They are not always necessary, but rather, they are placeholders for what we might be able to accomplish if we had zero fear, like skydiving or bungee jumping, or they may be so exaggerated as to be unreasonable, such as eating food off the floor.

There is no clinical reason to do your top exposure unless it is something that brings you joy or gives you a sense of accomplishment. Sometimes it is useful to push far past the OCD before settling on a more balanced approach. Other times, it is not necessary. A more compassionate approach to OCD treatment does not need to push exposures to their limits.

Plan Gradual, Measurable Exposures and Response Preventions

The number one mistake people make with ERP is doing exposures only one time and then moving on to the next exposure before their nervous system has had time to recover from the first. When in doubt, slow it down and repeat an exposure. In my ERP practice, I always err on the side of compassion and patience.

You will know you are ready to move to the next exposure when your brain is bored with the current step in the hierarchy. You will have repeated your current exposure to the point where your brain is over it. This process, called desensitization of fear, looks something like this:

Each practice round of the exposure will spark less fear. If you are not following up your exposures by engaging in compulsions, your brain will systematically desensitize. However, each person's process is unique to them. Some people need only two or three repetitions of an exposure to systematically desensitize, while others need more. If you are still having panic peaks after more than five repetitions of an exposure, then most likely you need to break that task down into smaller pieces or go back down to an earlier step in your hierarchy.

Now, let's say you have repeated an exposure sufficiently and you no longer feel fear-triggered by it. How long before you move on to your next exposure? Your nervous system needs time to recover between exposures. Ideally, you will want to get back down to your baseline level of anxiety before triggering an acute spike of fear.

Because many of us with OCD function at a high baseline level of anxiety in ordinary life, it can be hard to judge when we are having an exposure-related spike. Part of the problem is the ambiguity of the term "anxiety." We often use this term to describe feelings that may actually be overwhelm, stress, dread, fear, or even excitement. Remember, you are intentionally triggering fear as you move through your hierarchy. Fear is the short-lived adrenal response that comes from a perceived threat. As you proceed, it is important to not still be experiencing fear from the last step.

Pacing yourself well in ERP means you have both a desire to be courageous *and* a nonjudgmental acceptance of your limitations. I want you to forge ahead on your exposure hierarchy not because you *should* be at the next step, but because your nervous system has desensitized to the step you are on. You will know this is the case when you no longer feel triggered by that exposure.

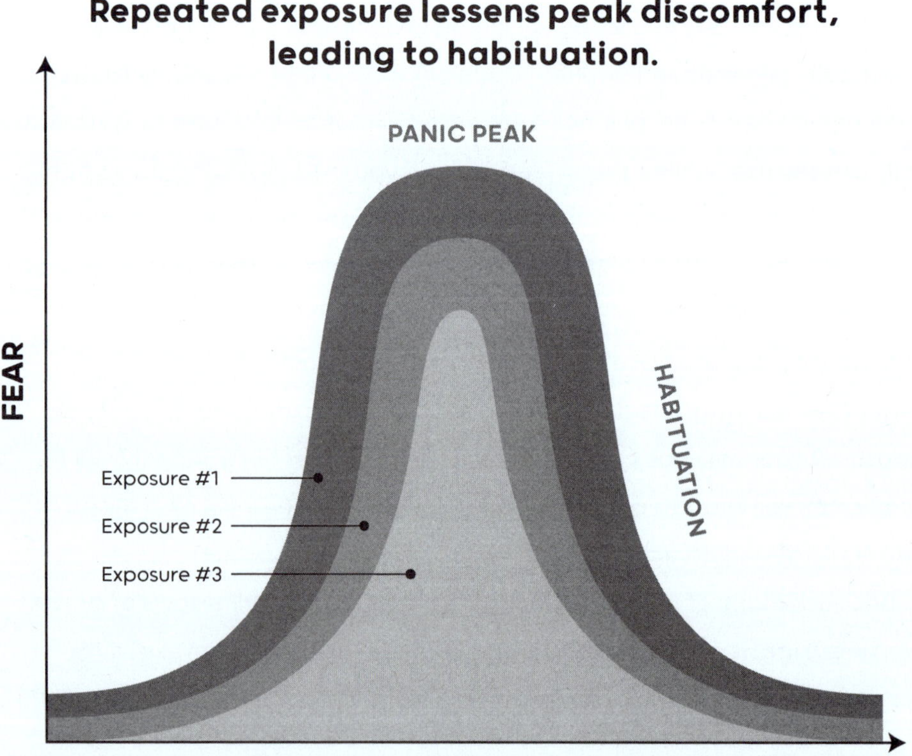

Figure Out Duration and Homework

OCD work can be time-consuming, but you will be rewarded for your investment. You can think of ERP like weight lifting—you see results when you consistently go to the gym and do multiple sets and reps spread out over time. If you overdo it one day, you might strain a muscle and need to take time off to recover.

When you are doing ERP for the first time, do no more than 30 minutes a day. After you've gained strength and confidence, perhaps you can do up to one hour of ERP a day. I never recommend much more than that. Just like with weight lifting, too many hours of the same exercise won't help you; it is how you get hurt.

Balance, patience, and consistency are key. I recommend that my clients set a daily alarm to practice ERP. That said, I am pleased when they tell me they turned off the alarm without practicing, as this shows they aren't approaching ERP work with rigidity. This alarm is an opportunity for you to tune into what you really need in each given moment, and sometimes, your ERP work is just not it.

You don't have to be hard on yourself to be consistent. True story: I spend only 20 minutes at the gym when I go. My teens make fun of me, but I have found that 20 minutes is the perfect amount of time and effort for me at this stage in my life. If I try to do more than 20 minutes, I will start avoiding it. But if I ask myself to do just 20 minutes, I will go most days and feel good about my progress. You get to define your pace. My only ask is that you keep moving forward.

Try Your First Exposure

Good news: If you are like most people, you have already done your first three significant exposures:

1. Opening this book
2. Reading about ERP
3. Creating an exposure hierarchy

Congratulate yourself for these massive accomplishments! It took me over a decade to take steps two and three. If this book had existed back when I could have used it, I might have walked right past it in the bookstore in favor of more soothing resources. You, however, have shown that you are ready for a challenge.

Now it is time to try an exposure from your exposure hierarchy. Choose one that takes five minutes or less and has a rating of three or lower. You are looking to spark some anxiety, but more important, to gain confidence. Here are some examples of my clients' successful first exposures:

- Close out one tab on my computer that I have open "just in case" or "as a reminder."
- Crack the knuckles on one hand and then sit with the discomfort for five minutes before letting myself crack the knuckles on my other hand.
- Break one small rule during a handwashing ritual (such as one less "Happy Birthday" or one less squirt of soap).
- Knock over a chair in my office and not say, "I'm sorry."
- Remove a compulsive app from my phone home page.

Sometimes people want their first exposure to be something they truly want to do but feel fear about doing it. These can be incredibly rewarding exposures—for example, going to salsa club for 10 minutes or having one delicious food that OCD tells you is unsafe or bad.

Regardless of what you choose for your first exposure, have compassion if you get stuck or feel more fear than you anticipated. Knowing how to push forward with self-compassion is part of this journey. If needed, go back to chapter 3 for grounding techniques to help you get through this step.

After you complete your first exposure, go back into your exposure hierarchy and note the actual SUDS next to your predicted SUDS (see page 96). You may need to revise your exposure hierarchy as you go to make it easier or more challenging, depending on how your exposures go in practice. The actual SUDS help you understand if anticipatory anxiety is misjudging the difficulty of your exposures.

Remember to celebrate your progress, even when you have taken just a single step. The "Exposure Gratitude Journal" on page 112 will help you honor your progress.

Monitor Progress

Track and analyze your progress without judgment. I suggest completing the "Progress Check-In Worksheet" (see page 106) every two weeks. Keep in mind that recovery isn't linear. Take a look:

You may err on the side of rushing through exposures, or you may delay them indefinitely. You may be pushing yourself too hard or letting yourself off the hook too often. You may be in an unconscious avoidance cycle. You may start out energized and dedicated, but then lose focus. At some point, you may even feel too little hope to go on. All these responses to ERP are normal.

If you notice any issues with progress, start with self-compassion: You are doing a hard thing. Accept your strong feelings, your worrisome thoughts, your exposure hiccups, and all the messiness that comes with a mental health healing journey. Next, reach out to your support network. Share your progress and your setbacks with your loved ones and other supporters. Sometimes OCD makes us feel uncomfortable asking for help—in that case, add it to your exposure hierarchy! Oftentimes, an accountability partner or even just an occasional cheerleader on the sidelines can make all the difference.

Also, remember that your exposure plan is a work in progress. In the next chapter, you will learn how to revise your exposure hierarchy based on your exposure experiences. As you move through this process, you will gain self-awareness and be able to revise your plan accordingly.

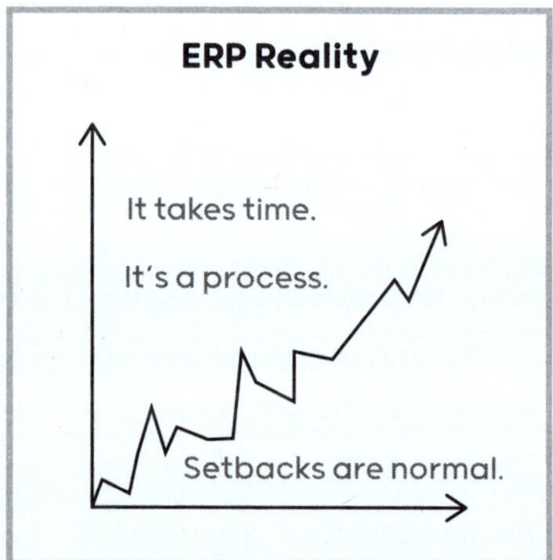

Work Through Your Remaining Fears

You know you are ready to move on to the next fear once you no longer feel activated by your exposures. My clients often start cracking jokes during exposures they previously found to be triggering. Sometimes, younger children will complain, "This exposure is getting so boring!" When you start to feel little or no anxiety during an exposure, your mind will probably start wandering. This is a sign you have sufficiently acclimated to the fear.

If you are not getting desensitized to your fears, even when you break them down into smaller, more manageable steps, it might be time to reach out to an OCD clinician. Not all fears can be handled through self-guided exposures.

Starting an exposure hierarchy can feel impossible, even with the best intentions. The anticipatory anxiety of a single exposure may be overwhelming, or we might struggle with executive function or depression, which can interfere with treatment. For some, beginning ERP can even trigger past trauma, which requires support before they can move forward. In these instances, having the structure of an OCD recovery program or a therapist is crucial to progress.

Progress Check-In Worksheet

Your exposure hierarchy will help you keep track of completed exposures with actual SUDS levels. This short worksheet is a nice add-on for biweekly reflections on your big-picture progress. You can use your ERP journal for subsequent biweekly reflections.

Answer the following questions with the past two weeks in mind:

1. What have you noticed about your overall anxiety level?

____

____

____

____

____

____

2. Describe your motivation levels. What has helped you find motivation?

____

____

____

____

____

____

3. Have you noticed any change in your willingness to do hard things? If yes, give examples.

4. What have you noticed around your compulsions? Are you doing fewer compulsions or any new compulsions?

5. How have your obsessions or intrusive thoughts shifted?

6. Are your major OCD themes consistent since the beginning of treatment or have they changed? If yes, explain.

Remember, these prompts have no right or wrong answers, only *your* answers. When you gain insight that something isn't working in your treatment, avoid self-blame. Successful ERP requires you to be honest with yourself. Compassionate ERP requires you to act kindly with your truth. Information gained through journaling and reflection can be used to revise your exposures and create a more sustainable exposure hierarchy. The best treatment plans are highly individualized and flexible.

Identify Resistance

This exercise is helpful when you can't move forward with the next exposure on your hierarchy because you are avoiding it, have lost motivation, or perhaps hopelessness has set in—in other words, you have been spiralizing down. In this exercise, you will purposefully explore your what-if fears until you reach the worst-case scenario to help you understand your resistance to an exposure. With this awareness and despite the anxiety, you can start back up the spiral by doing just one thing that moves you forward.

What exposure are you stuck on?

What do you think will happen if you do this exposure?

And then what?

And then what?

And then what?

And then what?

What would it mean about you if all these things happened?

Your answer to the last question probably revealed a core fear. By finding it, you can now compassionately recognize what is making you feel stuck on this exposure. This new insight also helps you gain perspective on the leaps your OCD is making and how disproportionately large they are–from a small exposure to a catastrophic fear. This can give you the motivation you need to move forward, despite the anxiety, in some small way.

Here is an example of how one of my clients responded to this exercise:

What exposure are you stuck on?

Not tipping the barista.

What do you think will happen if you do this exposure?

She will judge me.

And then what?

I will feel horrible.

And then what?

I won't be able to stop thinking about it.

And then what?

I will convince myself that I am a bad person.

And then what?

I will never feel good about myself ever again.

What would it mean about you if all these things happened?

That I will want to die.

In this example, my client realizes they are resisting people-pleasing exposures because they have a core fear they will become suicidal if they don't feel like a good person. When it is all laid out on the page like this, this client was able to compassionately acknowledge their core fear and move forward with the exposure despite their anxiety.

Spiraling Up versus Spiraling Down

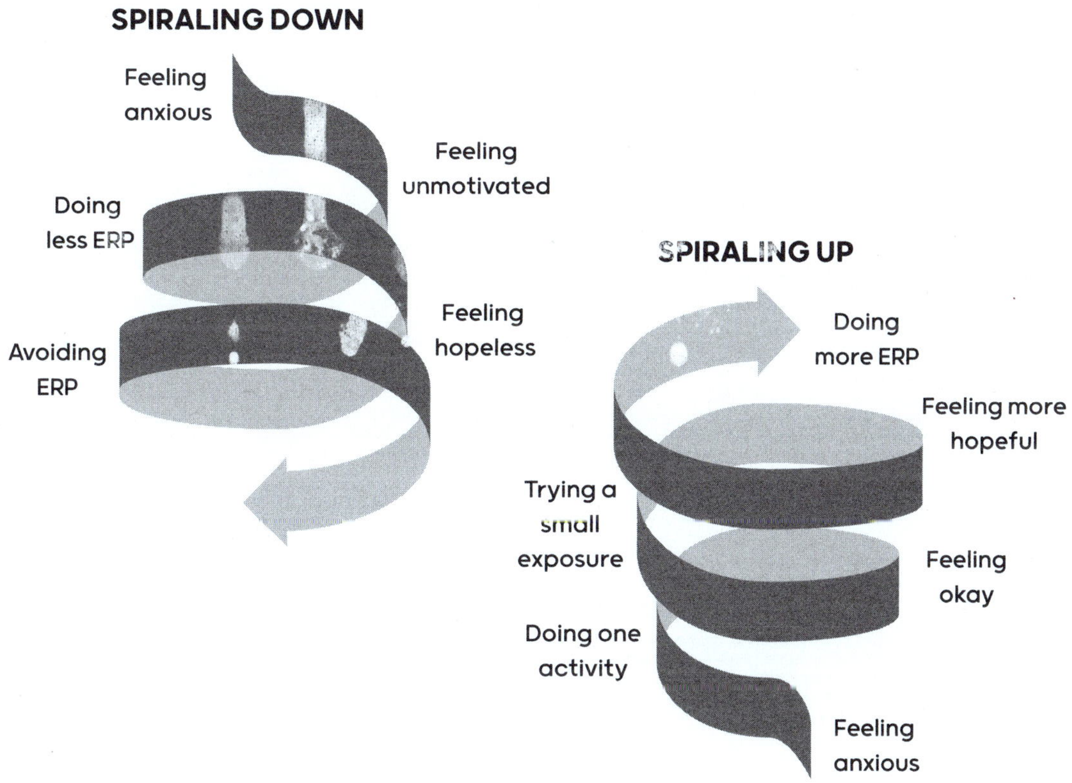

Exposure Gratitude Journal

This exercise guides you to express gratitude toward yourself for completing a difficult exposure. This journaling practice is especially valuable if you are dismissive of your ERP accomplishments—for example, "That wasn't a big deal" or "Other people do that all the time." You can learn to embrace self-kindness through journaling until it becomes more natural. Use your ERP journal for subsequent entries.

1. Write down the exposure you accomplished in bold letters.

    ____

2. Describe your experience of the exposure using one or more of these journal prompts:

    Where in your body did you feel this exposure?

    ____

    ____

    ____

    ____

    What thoughts and emotions did this exposure provoke?

    ____

    ____

    ____

    ____

How has accomplishing this task brought you closer to your goals?

If your exposure was to do a previously avoided activity, how long has it been since you did this task? Why is it significant that you committed to doing this task again?

After this accomplishment, what would you say to your past self?

3. After reflecting on the exposure through these prompts, spend one minute focusing on thanking yourself for doing this exposure. Note, with gratitude, that you experienced temporary discomfort to invest in your future self.

Someone Else's Exposure Hierarchy

This exercise is helpful if you feel stuck creating your own exposure hierarchy. After years of developing other people's exposure challenges, I can much more easily get my creative juices flowing with my own. We are more objective when it comes to someone else's fears. Also, this can be good practice for prioritizing compassion when designing your exposures.

1. Choose a family member or friend you love and admire and feel protective of. Think of what one of their fears may be.

2. Now create an exposure hierarchy that would help this person slowly build up to fully facing that fear.

3. Imagine this person doing each task on your list. How would they react? Where would they get stuck? How would you support them through each step?

4. Discuss: If possible, ask that person to look over the list and give you feedback on how to make it more manageable.

5. Bonus: If that person is interested, they may do one (or more) of the tasks on the exposure hierarchy to experience ERP and understand the work you are doing to heal.

Fear and Response Diary

Use this worksheet to log your fears and responses to help you track your progress. Respond to the journal prompts that follow once you have gathered some data. Use your ERP journal when you need more space.

Date/Time	Fear Trigger	Response to Fear
1/22/2025 9:00 p.m.	Heard a noise, had intrusive thought about a break-in	Opening up Furbo app to monitor living room, rechecking back door lock, rumination

Journal Prompts

How do my responses to my fears make me feel better in the moment?

How do my responses to my fears reinforce the fear in the long term?

How might I respond differently to my fears?

Sample O/C/I/F Doc Entries

Here are real-life examples of obsessions, compulsions, intrusive thoughts, and fear cycles borrowed from some of my clients' O/C/I/F docs. You can use these to help you categorize the entries you listed on your draft O/C/I/F doc (see page 88).

Obsessions

- Fear of suffering (health, comfort)
- Fear of catastrophic illness (son getting cancer, going through the process of cancer, rare illnesses or prolonged course of common illnesses, common infections that result in severe consequences or skin infections that result in amputations, things that go particularly badly)
- Fear of causing suffering for others
- Fear of being sick on an airplane or other captive space
- Fear of freak accidents/falls
- Fear of high-speed car accidents that result in death or lifelong traumatic brain injury
- Fear of terrorist events/random isolated targeting from bad actors
- Fear of vomiting
- Fear of having pleasure (because I will let my guard down)
- Fear of any avoidable suffering (mental or physical)

Compulsions

- Hypervigilance
- Rumination about when son got RSV at 18 months
- Mental replay to look for patterns/clues how I can better predict illness
- Recap journal so that I can find clues in the future if he gets sick or something bad happens
- Handwashing
- If anyone comes to the house, afterward bleach the bathroom, bleach common surfaces, wash anything they were on with bleach or sanitizing cycle on dishwasher or washer
- Masking as I can
- Overvigilance toward my phone
- Avoiding people with signs of illness (watching people, the way they are breathing, talking, eating, and asking, "Do they have a subclinical illness?")
- Three squirts of soap minimum
- Reading stories about terrible illnesses or freak accidents for clues on how to avoid such fates
- Preparing emergency plans (vomit-readiness bins, respiratory cart, hospital-transport plans, hiding plans, exit strategies, go bags, apocalypse prep, traveling with meds, stockpiling emergency meds)
- Avoidance of places I think are high-risk such as certain restaurants, trains, high-touch areas, areas with lots of children, and so forth

- Avoidance of activities when I feel off (tired, nauseated, possibility of a stomachache)
- Seeking reassurance from others, even if only in the form of comfort or empathy

Intrusive Thoughts

- *At any moment, my son's school will call and say he is sick or hurt.*
- *At any moment, my son could be getting exposed to something.*
- *I may have some terrible cancer lurking beneath the surface that will kill me and leave my son without me.*
- *Even common infections can have terrible consequences for some people.*
- *I should be learning more about the various threats and tracking them better.*
- *If I am experiencing joy, that is a form of non-vigilance or negligence, and I'm being naive to threats.*
- *Every good thing can and will come to an end, and pain is inevitable.*
- *My life has been too good thus far. Statistically, major pain or trauma is coming.*
- *I am going to snap and kill my family or do something radically negligent that results in major demise. Everyone will hate me, and I'll hate myself, and my life will be completely over.*
- *All it takes is one bad thing out of 10 million well-handled, responsible, good things for life to be ruined.*

Fear Cycles

- I hear my phone buzz; I feel an instant pang of worry. If I check my phone and there is nothing concerning, I mentally replay the morning drop-off at school to see if there was anything that happened that I need to worry about.
- I feel an unevenness in my leg; I have an intrusive thought that it might be a tumor. I google "leg cancer" and "tumors beneath the skin's surface." I ask ChatGPT. I ask my husband. He calms me down, but then I replay his words when I go to bed because I still need reassurance.
- I read a news article about flash floods. I start to think about the rivers in my town and which ones might have flooding dangers. I research what the city has done to mitigate the flood risk. After discovering that no mitigation has happened in the creek next to my son's school, I find the email of the government department in charge of flood risk, and I send an email asking for more information. I obsesses about this creek until at school pickup, when I see it in person and realize it is barely a foot of water.

These examples help to paint a clearer picture of how OCD operates in the real world. By using them as a guide, you can categorize your own experiences to better understand the unique patterns of your OCD and further strategize your compassionate ERP plan.

Tools to Adjust Your Exposure Plans

5

This chapter helps you troubleshoot your self-guided ERP with practical advice. As you move through your exposure hierarchy, it is okay to adjust your treatment plan. Exposure hierarchies can go through many iterations, especially if predicted SUDS and actual SUDS are widely different. Sometimes, you may learn that your exposure plan missed the mark and did not successfully target the OCD fear you are working on—or even that a new theme is more prevalent midway through and you need to come up with new exposures.

How to Adjust as Needed

When you look at the totality of an exposure hierarchy, you may feel intimidated by the more difficult exposures. Try not to look too far ahead and focus on the part of the exposure hierarchy you are facing today. Remember that you can always adjust or eliminate too difficult exposures once you reach that level in the treatment. Don't underestimate how much your perspective will change every week you spend facing your fears. You may discover that by the time you are near the end of the exposure hierarchy, the impossible feels possible.

But what if you are moving through the exposure hierarchy and you don't seem to be getting better? Yes, you may get temporarily desensitized to each individual part of the exposure hierarchy, but on a big-picture level, you might feel more anxious than ever. Short-term heightened anxiety is a sign that ERP is working! However, if you have long-term, sustained, or even worsened anxiety after one to two months of ERP, you may want to reconsider your treatment plan.

The ERP tools in this chapter are additional, nonmandatory sources of help. They include tools that are most applicable for certain subtypes, as well as tools that help you brainstorm exposures for tricky-to-treat forms of OCD.

Frequently Asked Questions

Here are some questions my clients frequently ask during ERP treatment. These focus on common bumps in the road. For more complex challenges, see chapter 6.

Question: Is it normal to be super tired after exposures?
Answer: Yes! Exposures require a sustained effort to process difficult emotions and resist the brain's desire to engage in compulsions. Exposures activate a physiological fear response that temporarily gives you more energy (i.e., a burst of adrenaline). However, this energy is short-lived; as you re-regulate, you may feel physically depleted. I have clients who take a nap after almost every difficult exposure.

Question: If I feel like I am over the fear, do I really have to finish everything on the exposure hierarchy?
Answer: Not necessarily. Remember, your exposure plan is yours to create and yours to terminate. If you feel you have met your treatment goals, the self-compassionate thing to do is move on. An ERP purist might push for higher-rated exposures to solidify your gains, but I don't believe that is necessary.

Question: What should I do if I can't stop my mental compulsions?
Answer: If your OCD is largely mental (i.e., pure O OCD), you may need more practice in mindfulness. You cannot stop intrusive thoughts or images, but you do have a certain level of control over mental compulsions. You can develop even more control over mental compulsions with

patience and practice. The skills in chapter 3—distress tolerance, cognitive defusion, and emotional distancing—can help.

Question: What if something bad happens during exposures that reinforces my fears?
Answer: Wait a few days and then do an easier exposure, working your way back up to that exposure. Unfortunately, in life, sometimes an unlikely feared outcome happens. Maybe, for example, we get into a minor accident during a driving exposure, we get a cold when we are practicing less frequent handwashing, or a food exposure makes us vomit. While it is far less likely to happen than OCD predicts, bad things occasionally happen that make compulsions and avoidance seem justified. The key here is to carry on as planned. OCD may convince us otherwise, but we *can* cope if something bad happens.

Question: Should I try again if I got emotionally flooded during an exposure?
Answer: Not yet. First, re-regulate using some of the strategies in chapter 3 to activate your parasympathetic nervous system. Then use the "What Went Wrong?" journaling exercise on page 127 to try to identify factors that contributed to the overexposure. Compassionate ERP puts more emphasis on trying to minimize flooding events. However, due to the variability of the human brain and mood, we cannot always avoid it. I suggest you try the exposure again once you re-regulate, but perhaps modify it first to make it a little less difficult.

"What Went Wrong?" Journaling Prompts

Every setback is a learning opportunity. To help you prevent similar experiences and improve future exposures, use these prompts to analyze an exposure that pushed you too far. Try to stay in a judgment-free zone. Reviewing what happened during a difficult exposure might bring back anxious emotions, but it will help you process what happened and move on.

Before you begin, take a few mindful breaths, feeling into the expansion and releasing as you inhale and exhale. If your breathing gets shallow as you respond to the prompts, stop writing and redirect your attention to the present moment. When you feel present, resume. Take mindful breaths throughout this exercise to help clear your mind and stay in the here and now.

1. Describe the events of the day leading up to the difficult exposure. What challenges did you face? What was your overall mood?

2. Write out everything you remember about the exposure and the subsequent flooding event. If you experienced panic, describe how it felt in your body.

3. Can you remember any intrusive thoughts you had during the exposure or directly after?

4. How did you re-regulate after your panic? What helped? What didn't help?

5. What other factors do you think were at play to worsen your experience during that exposure?

6. Brainstorm three strategies you could integrate into this exposure to improve your experience (e.g., doing this exposure with a therapy animal).

7. Reread the earlier exposures in your exposure hierarchy. How did they prepare you for this exposure? How did they fall short?

8. Revise your exposure hierarchy to minimize the possibility of a second flooding event while still helping you move forward in your exposure plan.

After completing this exercise, revise your exposure hierarchy. Feel free to move down the hierarchy to repeat your last successful exposure before repeating this one. Remember, OCD treatment is about continuity, patience, and mastery . . . not speed!

Exposure Cheat Sheet for Common Fears

The exposure hierarchies provided here are meant as examples, created by and for others. If you share one of these fears, you can choose to use that particular exposure hierarchy, but first, be sure to rank and rate each exposure based on how hard it would be for *you*.

People-Pleasing Exposure Plan

- Saying no at work to a customer/client. 2
- Not calling someone back. 2
- Saying no over email. 3
- Saying no to a request from a family member. 4
- Saying no to an extra task for school, work, or a club. 5
- Not volunteering when a volunteer is requested. 6
- Not matching someone's enthusiasm about an activity/plan. 6
- Saying no to going out when others want to. 6
- Asking someone else to do you a favor. 7
- Not apologizing when I don't do something that others want. 8
- Canceling a commitment without giving a reason. 9
- Saying no to a friend who wants something. 9
- Hanging up on someone rudely. 9
- Not driving when the light turns green until another car honks. 10

Fear of Contamination Exposure Plan

- Listening to a news story about people getting sick. 4
- Touching a public keyboard without washing my hands right after. 5
- Eating food that dropped on the ground in my house. 5
- Throwing out disinfectant wipes. 5
- Touching someone else's dog and then not washing my hands. 5
- Going to sit on a park bench and then sitting on the sofa. 5
- Touching the ground at the doctor's office. 6
- Eating something that dropped on the ground outside. 7
- Eating something with my hands without washing them first. 6
- Only decontaminating the phone once a week. 7
- Eating in public without handwashing before. 7
- Going into the ER waiting room and then not washing my hands. 8
- Not showering for a full day. 8
- Sitting in a public place and then climbing into bed in the same clothes. 8
- Touching a menu and then eating food with my hands. 9
- Never decontaminating the phone. 9

Fear of Blood Exposure Plan

- Writing a story about getting blood in my food and eating it. 1
- Putting a red marker stain on shirt or sheets. 2
- Eating a red Skittle and saying aloud, "This is a scab of blood." 3
- Watching a fictional video with real-looking fake blood. 3
- Licking a red cupcake and imagining I am licking blood. 4
- Eating a plum and saying, "I'm biting into flesh." 4
- Putting fake blood on the kitchen counter. 5
- Looking at a real photo of a person getting a blood draw. 5
- Eating a meal with edible fake blood on top. 6
- Watching a surgeon's instructional video with real blood. 7
- Watching a YouTube video about HIV in blood. 8
- Doing a finger prick and getting one drop of blood. 9
- Going to a blood donation event. 10
- Volunteering at a hospital. 10

Fear of Needles Exposure Plan

- Talking about needles. 1
- Drawing a needle. 2
- Looking at a cartoon drawing of a needle. 2
- Looking at a still photo of a needle. 3
- Looking at my inner arm for 10 minutes and imagining a blood draw. 3
- Looking at a real picture of a vaccine going into someone's arm. 4
- Looking at a real picture of a blood draw. 4
- Watching a video of a needle being held and moved around in the flesh. 5
- Looking at a real needle. 5
- Holding a real needle with the cap on. 6
- Visiting the blood draw station at a hospital. 6
- Holding a real needle with the cap off. 7
- Using a needle to inject an orange. 7
- Watching a video of someone getting a blood draw. 7
- Watching someone else get an injection in person. 8
- Getting an immunization shot. 9
- Getting blood drawn with numbing cream. 10
- Getting blood drawn without numbing cream. 10

An Angry Letter to My OCD

In this activity, you will name and externalize your OCD and try to manifest some anger toward it. You may be so used to blaming and shaming yourself that you forgot your OCD is external to your true self. You will need a quiet, reflective space, stationery or lined paper, and at least 45 minutes to drop in, reflect, write, and re-regulate. This is a good exercise for when you don't feel motivated to do your exposures.

1. **Name your OCD.** I named mine Pani Truszkowska–a strict Polish matron in my imagination. You can pick any name or character that fits your OCD's energy, whether it is a fictious villain or monster. Ideally, this name should evoke a clear image. Feel free to be silly. Some names my clients have chosen include Alien, Meanie, Captain Ahab (from *Moby Dick*), Joan (from *Mommie Dearest*), Miranda (from *The Devil Wears Prada*), and Lady Macbeth (from Shakespeare's *Macbeth*).

2. **Bring to mind how your OCD has impacted you.** How has it held you back? What has it taken from you? Tap into some righteous anger toward your OCD, and let that emotion rise inside you for a moment.

3. **Now compose a letter addressed to your OCD using the name you came up with.** Keep that image in mind as you write. Take no mercy! Rip into the OCD for manipulating you into engaging in compulsions, holding you back, and striking fear into your heart. You are lashing out at the OCD, not at yourself.

4. **After you sign the letter, take a moment to get resettled in your body by taking a few breaths.** Imagine the surge of anger receding like a wave into a gentle froth.

5. **Now sit on the ground with your hands resting on your knees, palms facing up.** (In dialectical behavior therapy, this pose is called *willing hands.*) Close your eyes and picture your exposure plan. Visualize yourself fighting back against the OCD villain. See yourself welcoming in the exposure plan because it will help you get your freedom back.

   TIP: You may want to reread this letter in moments when you are stuck or want to keep obeying the OCD. Look at it when your brain is telling you that your OCD is reasonable.

Perfectionism Interference Worksheet

Certain forms of perfectionism can interfere with your ability to move forward with your exposure plan. If you identify as a perfectionist, complete this general perfectionism assessment and then complete the reflective journal prompts that follow.

How often do you experience the following?	Not At All	Somewhat	Often	Notes
Rigidity about how tasks should be completed	❑	❑	❑	
Need for control over projects	❑	❑	❑	
Fear of making a mistake	❑	❑	❑	
Aversion to activities at which you do not excel	❑	❑	❑	
Avoidance of starting a new or difficult task	❑	❑	❑	
Fear of disapproval from an authority figure	❑	❑	❑	
Difficulty choosing the right words	❑	❑	❑	
Difficulty collaborating with others	❑	❑	❑	
Need for things to be consistent	❑	❑	❑	
Focus on excellence	❑	❑	❑	
Feeling the need to be productive	❑	❑	❑	

How often do you experience the following?	Not At All	Somewhat	Often	Notes
Fear of falling behind	❑	❑	❑	
Rereading for fear of having missed something	❑	❑	❑	
Not completing tasks out of fear of doing them inadequately	❑	❑	❑	
Rumination over past errors	❑	❑	❑	

Journal Prompts

What does the saying "Perfect is the enemy of the good" mean to you, and how does it apply to your experience of self-guided ERP so far?

Think of one specific instance when your brain labeled an ERP task or activity as a failure. Reflect on the emotions and behaviors that followed.

How could you have reframed this "failure" as a growth opportunity? What would you have gained by celebrating this difficult moment as a positive step?

Your Self-Compassionate Progress Report

1. Respond to these three prompts to journal your successes:

   Name three brave moments in your ERP journey so far.

   Describe how you overcame an obstacle in your ERP plan.

How have you surprised yourself in your ERP work?

2. Use one of these three options to accentuate and celebrate your successes:

   Option 1: Share one of these three brave moments with a loved one, a support group member, or even post it on a public forum that celebrates exposure therapy. My Instagram @letstalk.ocd is an incredibly positive space where followers often uplift each other in the comments of my posts.

   Option 2: Compose a loving affirmation for yourself that celebrates your courage in the face of fear—for example, *I have a well of courage within me. I am bravely facing uncertainty. At my core, I am strong.* Use Post-it notes to display this affirmation in your home, especially on mirrors, where you might be examining and reflecting on yourself.

   Option 3: Listen to a guided meditation on YouTube. Keywords to search for are "strength," "courage," and "bravery." Remember to not misuse this resource, as it is easy to get sucked in when you open the app.

Figuring Out Difficult Challenges

6

Everyone who embarks on ERP faces challenges along the way. This chapter explores some of the most significant challenges that may arise during self-guided ERP. Setbacks are an invitation to practice self-compassion and refocus on your individual needs. Above all, do not let go of hope, as hope is a precious ingredient in this work. These challenges can feel unmanageable in the moment, but with guidance and patience, healing is possible. After every setback, you can continue to choose ERP.

When the Road Gets Rocky

The challenges faced when you are trying self-guided ERP are as varied and unique as OCD itself. Here is a short list of the ones I see most commonly:

- Low motivation
- Barriers due to neurodiversity
- Unhealthy environments that interfere with healing
- Reliance on actions (safety behaviors) to prevent a feared outcome
- A belief that the OCD is right
- Expecting too much too soon
- Lack of distress tolerance skills

For certain subtypes of OCD, ERP can be derailed in specific ways. For example, the normal ebbs and flows of a relationship, including disagreements, can interfere with treatment for relationship OCD. You might be making progress on your exposure hierarchy only to encounter a true relationship hurdle that shakes your faith in the relationship. When this happens, the confusion between OCD and reality can stall your progress.

Similarly, a medical diagnosis, or even an out-of-the-norm physical symptom, can derail health OCD progress. Sometimes your specific fears around your health will shift in the middle of ERP. You may have designed an exposure hierarchy around fear of cancer, but suddenly, all you can think about is your new symptom and a new disease. In this case, you need to pivot your OCD work to focus on the here-and-now fears.

Most commonly, however, human nature is the biggest challenge of self-guided ERP. The human body and brain are designed to protect us from harm and danger. Without an outside perspective, it is easier to view

OCD triggers as true danger. It can be incredibly difficult to willingly push yourself into a danger zone. You are only trying to keep yourself safe, and perhaps ERP does not *feel* safe to you. If this is the case, practice self-compassion skills. Go back to chapter 2 to try to realign with your reasons for choosing ERP.

Challenge: You Have Low Motivation for ERP

Low motivation during ERP happens to nearly everyone. It is often the product of avoidance and hopelessness. The former is a compulsion, and the latter is a limiting belief. The two reinforce each other. The more we avoid, the less hope we feel.

Don't underestimate the destructive nature of avoidance. We like to think of avoidance as a benign coping strategy (e.g., *I don't really need to do that thing; it's fine*), but it can hurt us quite deeply. Long-term avoidance fuels fear and makes the process of ERP even more difficult. After years of living with OCD, avoidance can become so ingrained that we barely notice it.

Similarly, you may have high motivation to learn about OCD but low motivation to apply what you have learned. Perhaps you will read this book cover to cover, but your OCD says you aren't ready to do any of the exercises. If that resonates with you, start by completing just one worksheet. That is all it takes.

Solutions

Low motivation is best solved by behavioral activation. Rather than trying to think your way into more motivation, you break avoidance patterns first. Behavioral activation means that you focus on replacing inaction with action, and even action that is somewhat unrelated to your OCD recovery. Starting with a fun activity can break up stuck feelings. If that goes well, then you can link an ERP activity to that fun activity. This is called behavioral chaining.

While instilling hope is important, one of the most tangible ways to gain hope is to *act* in a hopeful way. In other words, you may need to fake it until you make it. Focus on what you can and will do, rather than on how you are feeling. Your feelings are real, but at some point, they are not helping you move forward. Complete the "Steps Forward Planner" on page 153 to refocus on what you *can* accomplish.

When you are struggling with low motivation, don't forget to reward yourself for even the smallest actions. Recalibrate your expectations and celebrate even a little victory.

While doing research for this book, I found a workbook I had purchased a decade ago: *The Anxiety and Worry Workbook: The Cognitive Behavioral Solution*, by David A. Clark and Aaron T. Beck. I know I read it multiple times, but I had filled out only a single exercise. Even with just one worksheet, one action, I was on my way to healing.

Challenge: A Stressful Life Event Occurs

A stressful life incident, especially one that is related to your OCD theme, can spark a massive and sudden relapse. You may even feel like you are back to square one in your progress. The reason this type of relapse happens is because, at its core, OCD is trying to protect us. Whenever something stressful or traumatic happens, OCD uses the opportunity for its version of an "I told you so." Thankfully, this relapse only *feels* permanent.

If you process the trauma of the experience and get back to facing your fears, the surge will abate.

When I was in recovery for my harm OCD, my son had a severe sledding accident, which I was present for but failed to prevent. I started having intrusive images of his face after the crash. My brain would replay the sound of his scream. My compulsions came roaring back. My son recovered well after a minor surgery, but my OCD felt like it was snowballing. My key mistake was allowing my OCD free rein while I was in crisis mode directly after the accident. As many of us do, I reverted to what was familiar. Now I have solutions.

Solutions

When life throws you a curve ball, start with these five steps:

1. Spend time attending to your nervous system (without doing compulsions) by re-regulating and being aware of your body.
2. Seek support from others to process your difficult experience.
3. Notice what OCD wants you to do in response to your dysregulation.
4. Resist complying with the OCD, even temporarily, to avoid a relapse.
5. Refocus on your exposure hierarchy, even if it is harder to do.

As always, I urge you to take these steps mindfully and compassionately. You may not have the same resilience you had before the incident, and you may need to return to chapter 3 to rebuild your distress tolerance. Be patient with yourself and do not give up hope. You have not returned to square one. Recovery from relapse is far easier than your initial recovery. If you have not yet relapsed, but are afraid you might, use the "Stressful Life Event Relapse Prevention Worksheet" on page 156.

After my son's sledding accident, I needed to redo items from my original harm OCD exposure hierarchy. Opening the floodgates to my classic compulsions reinforced my old obsessions. I also had some new themes in my OCD that focused on harm associated with going downhill quickly. When OCD develops a new focus, we need to pivot our treatment plan. I added exposures to high water slides, sledding, and downhill biking.

Challenge: Depression Gets in the Way

Research suggests that between 25 and 50 percent of OCD experiencers also meet the criteria for clinical depression. OCD onset usually comes first, suggesting that depression could be the brain's response to the OCD. Depression is characterized by feelings of hopelessness, low self-esteem, desire to isolate, irritability, and lack of interest in activities that were previously engaging. Like OCD, depression tends to ebb and flow. Some experiencers report that when the OCD abates, the depression sets in (and vice versa). But, more commonly, the depression is present with the OCD; after all, being stuck in rumination and avoidance can take a lot of joy out of our lives.

Solutions

The concurrence of depression and OCD is one of the reasons this book is a *compassionate* guide to ERP. Infusing self-compassion throughout your OCD journey goes a long way toward encouraging gentleness, self-love, and self-forgiveness, qualities that depression does not want you to have. Never underestimate the power of taking a compassionate step back from the difficult work and caring for yourself.

In my clinical experience, depression also interferes with these four crucial ingredients in the ERP soup:

1. Persistence (aka stick-to-it-ness)
2. Hope
3. Positive belief in self
4. Ability to celebrate wins

Dr. Jonathan Abramowitz, an imminent scholar in the field of OCD, focused years of research on how to help those who experience both disorders. His conclusion was that ERP must be interwoven with cognitive behavioral therapy (CBT) to help experiencers develop a more positive view of the future and themselves. CBT is a therapeutic model based on the idea that people's emotions, body sensations, and behaviors stem from their perception of the world and events. Therefore, the objective truth of our lives does not matter as much as how we perceive it.

In CBT, automatic thoughts are the knee-jerk ways in which we think about ourselves and the world, which drive how we interact and feel. For example, if you hit a roadblock in ERP, the negative lens of depression might produce these automatic thoughts: *I can't do this, I am going to fail, This is too hard for me,* and *I should give up.* With depression, the negative lens gets even thicker. The initial interpretation of a setback can be deeply pessimistic. This lens directly affects persistence and hope. Conversely, if we are having ERP success, we may not even bother to celebrate wins because we believe that "we should be able to do that already."

CBT challenges us to notice the ways in which we distort the world through our depression lens and not to accept automatic thoughts as truth. Check out the "ERP Thought-Challenging Worksheet" on page 159 for a step-by-step guide for moments when depressive thinking is getting in the way of your ability to engage in ERP. Consider getting support for your depression alongside engaging in ERP work. Most of all, take a compassionate step back and ask yourself what you most need to heal in this moment.

The ERP will be here when you are ready. While it waits, I encourage you to speak with your healthcare provider about your depression.

Challenge: When OCD Meets Neurodiversity

The connection between OCD and neurodiversity is a subject that is still being explored. Right now, all we can say for sure is that a person with OCD is far more likely than others to also have some type of neurodiversity. For instance, more than 30 percent of people with OCD also meet the criteria for attention-deficit/hyperactivity disorder (ADHD). Recent studies have found that people with OCD are up to 13 times more likely to have autism spectrum disorder (ASD) than the general population.

Researchers are chasing down many theories for why this strong link exists. Some scientists hypothesize that certain genes must predispose us to both neurodiversity and OCD, and that neurodiversity comes in clusters. Others believe that mental health labels are far too simplistic, and the same neurobiological factors underly all these diagnoses. Suffice it to say, the frequent co-occurrence of OCD and neurodiversity is a reality. We cannot ignore the complexities our unique brains bring to exposure therapy.

As a neurodiversity-affirming clinician and a neurodiverse individual, I believe that many neurodiverse traits, such as creativity, passion, and dynamic thinking, can improve ERP outcomes. However, since this section is focused on roadblocks, let's look at some possible traits of ASD and ADHD that might hinder self-guided ERP. Keep in mind, however, that neurodiversity is unique to each individual, and no one fits fully into any category.

Common Traits of ASD and ADHD That May Impact ERP

ASD	ADHD
Difficulty with transitions	Impulsivity
Rigidity of habits	Distractibility
Sensory sensitivities	Rejection sensitivity
Difficulty labeling emotions	Hyperactivity
Overlap between ASD and OCD triggers	Difficulty with delayed gratification
Low distress tolerance	Low patience
Difficulty with change	Strong emotional reactions
Overattention to detail	Inattention to detail
Emotional overwhelm	Disorganization
Rule-following tendencies	Task avoidance

Solutions

The solution here is a redoubled emphasis on mindfulness. Mindfulness opens the door for self-compassion and accommodations for your neurodiversity. No one understands your neurodiversity better than you do. If you take the time to tap into it, you probably have good instincts about what you can handle and what you need to modify.

Similarly, only you can draw the line between what is a facet of your OCD and what is inherently you. Especially with ASD, it can be confusing to understand what aspect of your brain has been activated by a trigger. For example, misophonia can be a symptom of both ASD and OCD. This is a strong, negative emotional or physiological response to specific, everyday sounds, such as the sound of people chewing. You can be doing everything right in ERP, but the symptoms may appear treatment resistant. This is because ASD and ADHD symptoms do not respond to exposure therapy.

Hold compassion for the uniqueness of your brain. ERP is not a one-size-fits-all process. Adapt any exercise in this workbook to better suit your needs. You are not tied down to any of the guidelines you read here, and you can follow any path that works for you. If you have feedback on what works for your type of neurodiversity, please contact me via my Instagram @letstalk.ocd or my website, kairoswellnesscollective.com, and share it with me for my next book!

If you are unsure about whether you are experiencing neurodiversity, fill out the "Neurodiversity Inventory" on page 162.

Steps Forward Planner

To help you get past a block in your ERP process, I will share how behavioral activation helped me overcome occasional bouts with writer's block. Like most authors, I sometimes get stuck in front of a blank page. This feeling of inaction wrecks my motivation. I can't think my way out of it. I can't complain my way out of it. *I must write my way out of it.*

So first I find a preferred activity that is relatively low effort but high reward. For me, this is walking to my favorite café in town and treating myself to a hot matcha. The walk cuts through a nature preserve and past a beautiful little pond. Rather than stare at my laptop in despair, I pack it up and take it with me on this preferred activity.

After my walk and taking a sip of my overpriced matcha, I am ready to bring out my laptop again and try writing. If I can't write my book, I write something unrelated. But, most important, I am doing the action rather than thinking about the action. This is what behavioral activation is all about. Now it's your turn!

1. Briefly describe where and how you have gotten stuck with ERP.

2. How has it felt to be stuck with ERP?

____

____

____

____

____

____

3. What is your motivation to take steps forward?

____

____

____

____

____

____

4. Fill out the "Steps Forward Planner" on the next page. Include three fun activities, three simple exposures that you could do anywhere/anytime, and five rewards for the five days you will be taking steps forward. You will commit each day to interweaving fun actions with uncomfortable actions.

Steps Forward Planner

Three activities that I love . . .	
1	
2	
3	

Three ERP Tasks	
1	
2	
3	

Action Plan

STEP 5

STEP 4

STEP 3

STEP 2

STEP 1

REWARDS	1	2	3	4

Stressful Life Event Relapse Prevention Worksheet

1. Describe the stressful life event.

____

____

____

____

____

____

2. Circle some of the negative emotions you have had in response to this stressful life event.

Alarmed	Embarrassed	Hurt
Angry	Exhausted	Irritated
Annoyed	Fearful	Jealous
Ashamed	Frozen	Let Down
Crushed	Frustrated	Lost
Dejected	Guilty	Moody
Desperate	Heavy	Nervous
Diminished	Helpless	Numb
Disgusted	Hesitant	Out of Control

Overwhelmed	Resentful	Terrified
Panicky	Scared	Unappreciated
Powerless	Shocked	Unsure
Punished	Sorrowful	Worried
Rejected	Suspicious	

3. What does OCD want you to do in reaction to this stressful life event?

____

____

____

____

____

____

4. Given what you have learned in this book, what would likely happen if you did what OCD wanted?

____

____

____

____

____

____

5: **Try this visualization meditation:** *Sit comfortably on a soft chair or lie on the floor. Feel the ground against your feet or holding your full body. Close your eyes, and imagine yourself carrying on with ERP, just as you had before the stressful event. Visualize yourself successfully continuing through the exposure hierarchy and bravely propelling forward with your life. Celebrate this future version of yourself. Express gratitude toward future you's bravery and strength. When you are ready, open your eyes and return to this worksheet.*

6. Commit to one brave act from your exposure hierarchy.

   Today I pledge to:

   ____

   ____

   ____

   ____

   ____

   ____

ERP Thought-Challenging Worksheet

As you have learned, thoughts are not facts. Your perception of an experience and of yourself influences how you will think about your progress through ERP. OCD can create a negative lens on the world and ourselves, causing us to see situations as far more dangerous than they are and ourselves as less than we are. When our brain perceives a trigger, it produces a negative thought, which leads to feelings of fear and a compulsive need to fix the "problem." Take a look:

The Negative Lens

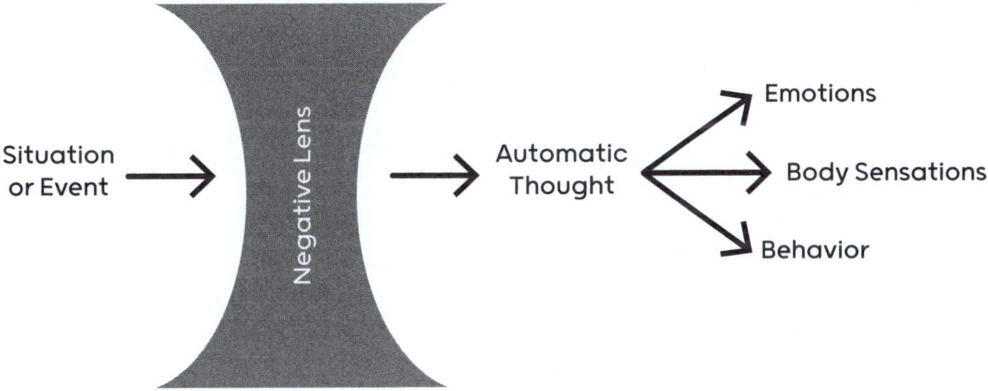

1. Identify your negative beliefs about yourself and your ability to engage in ERP. Here is an example: *This is too hard for me, and I don't have it in me.*

____

____

____

____

____

____

2. Review this list of cognitive distortions and check the boxes for any that might be influencing your beliefs.

- ☐ All-or-nothing thinking (e.g., *If I can't do all my exposures, I am a total failure.*)
- ☐ Emotional reasoning (e.g., *I feel bad, so I must not be doing it right.*)
- ☐ Labeling (e.g., *I am weak.*)
- ☐ Magnification/minimization (e.g., *My ERP setbacks are huge; my wins are tiny.*)
- ☐ Mental filter (e.g., *All I can think about is my anxiety, not my progress.*)
- ☐ Mind reading (e.g., *Others think I am not making progress.*)
- ☐ Overgeneralization (e.g., *I couldn't do that exposure, so I won't succeed with others.*)
- ☐ Predicting the future (e.g., *I will never be able to get over my OCD.*)
- ☐ *Should* statements (e.g., *I should be able to do these exposures easily*)

3. Try to look at your ERP experience from a positive lens.

If you were not using the cognitive distortions you checked off, how would you see your ERP journey?

How would you talk to your friend if they were in your position?

How would you engage differently with ERP if you saw it from this perspective?

What would be a good, positive step to take right now?

Neurodiversity Inventory

This inventory is a starting point to help you figure out if you might be neurodivergent. Answer yes or no in response to the following questions:

		Yes	No
1	Do you find your mind wandering when you are reading or listening to a presentation?	❑	❑
2	Do you significantly struggle with follow-through?	❑	❑
3	Do you feel that you learn differently from others?	❑	❑
4	Are you hyperaware of sounds, smells, and textures?	❑	❑
5	Do you tend to notice details other people miss?	❑	❑
6	Do you tend to miss obvious things other people see?	❑	❑
7	Do you have difficulty communicating how you feel?	❑	❑
8	Do you struggle with extreme procrastination?	❑	❑
9	Do you tend to hyperfocus on your interests?	❑	❑
10	Are you overstimulated in certain environments?	❑	❑
11	Do you feel like it is hard to fit in with others?	❑	❑

		Yes	No
12	Do you find yourself approaching problems from a unique angle?	❑	❑
13	Were you often called sensitive as a child?	❑	❑
14	Do you engage in repetitive behavior that is not related to OCD?	❑	❑
15	Do you feel the need to express excitement physically through hand or body movement?	❑	❑
16	Do you find that you need a long time to recover after social experiences?	❑	❑
17	Have you struggled to maintain or deepen relationships due to misunderstandings?	❑	❑
	Total		

Tally up the number of *yes* responses. If you answered yes to seven or more of these questions, consider reaching out to a psychiatrist or neuropsychologist for an assessment. If you are neurodivergent, it simply means your brain works differently from what is considered typical.

CONCLUSION
Maintenance and Relapse Prevention

Congratulations! You have done incredible work. I hope that you have already found measurable relief from your OCD. If you are still working through your exposure hierarchy, keep at it. Celebrate your progress at every step—not just when you finish.

Now let's talk maintenance and relapse prevention. Maintenance does not come naturally for most. OCD will relentlessly try to regain control. Relapse or even just a slip are a completely normal part of OCD recovery. You will likely need to keep facing fears and resisting compulsions, especially when your OCD refocuses on a new theme. Fortunately, ERP is like riding a bike. You may find yourself casually doing exposures without significant effort. I often think to myself, *My OCD just activated; I should lean into that fear.* Once you create those neural pathways of facing fears and disregarding intrusive thoughts, you can coast through a variety of situations without regressing to compulsions.

Life, however, is unpredictable. Sometimes there will be obstacles. Sometimes we will fall off the bike. In that case, it is important to go back to the knowledge that got you out of your OCD patterns the first time. Try to avoid all-or-nothing thinking traps such as, *ERP didn't work; the OCD is back.* You might only need a touch-up to get back to cruising.

When relapse happens, reground yourself in the books, your support system, and techniques that worked for you. A new theme does not usually need a new approach, just a modified version of the work you have already done. Remember to have faith in your inherent ability to heal. You have done so before, and you will do so again!

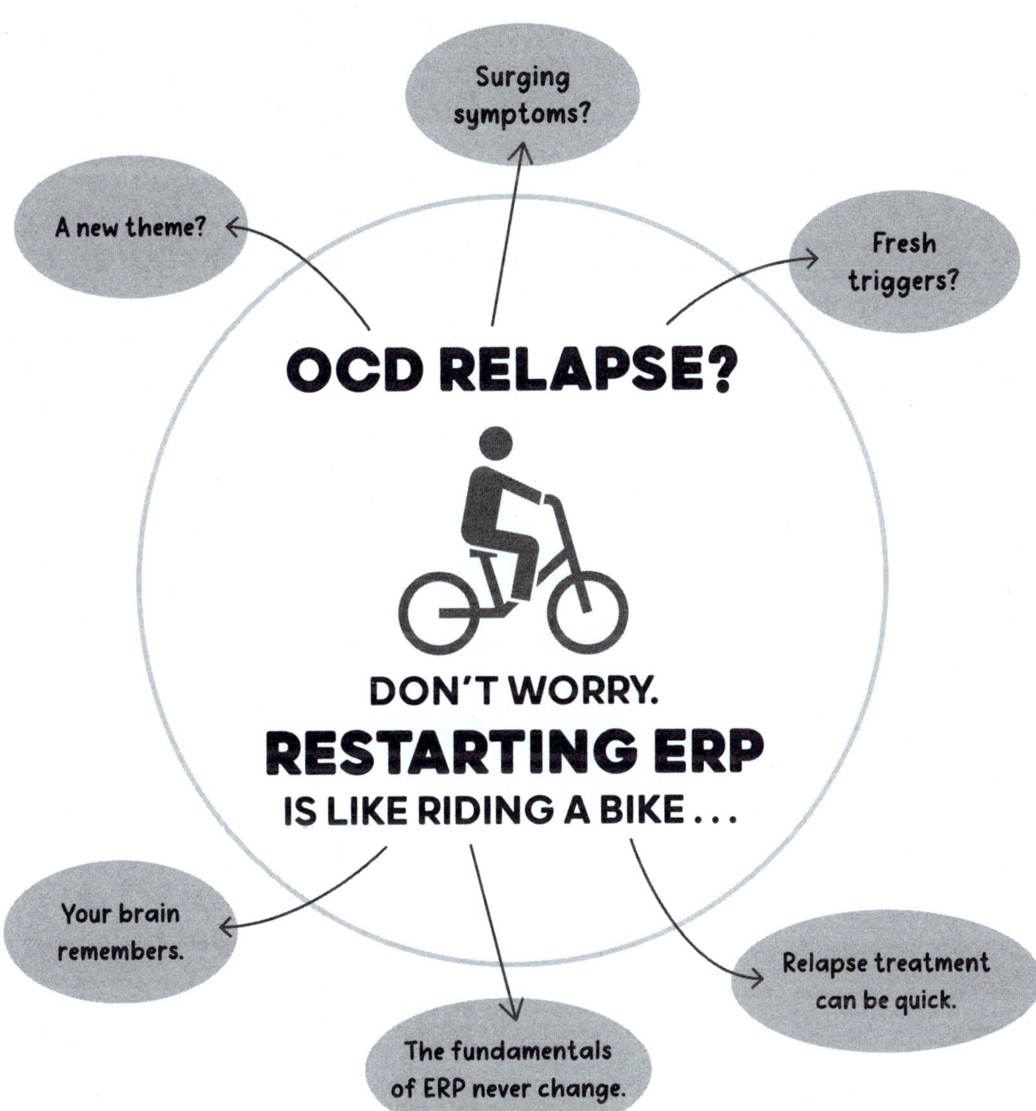
Surging symptoms?
A new theme?
Fresh triggers?
OCD RELAPSE?
DON'T WORRY.
RESTARTING ERP
IS LIKE RIDING A BIKE . . .
Your brain remembers.
Relapse treatment can be quick.
The fundamentals of ERP never change.

RESOURCES

Recommended Websites

The International OCD Foundation: iocdf.org

The IOCDF website is the most helpful accumulation of resources currently available on OCD and related disorders, such as hoarding and specific phobias. The website has an extensive directory of providers of OCD therapy organized by state and nation.

Not Alone Notes: notalonenotes.org

This nonprofit shares resources and hope for OCD recovery through a network of supportive volunteers. Experiencers mail notes to each other to encourage a sense of connection, even when face-to-face contact with others isn't possible.

Anxiety and Depression Association of America: adaa.org

This organization has a core mission of connecting experiencers to therapists and resources, as well as providing advanced training for clinicians. Visit this website for a trained therapist directory, peer-to-peer support groups, and information about emerging treatments for OCD, depression, and anxiety disorders.

***Beyond the Doubt* Blog: psychologytoday.com/us/blog/beyond-the-doubt**

A highly relatable blog series on *Psychology Today* helps universalize some of the struggles of OCD recovery. Authors and advocates Jeff Bell and Shala Nicely write about the very real doubts people have when they are going through ERP.

Recommended Reading

The Anxiety and Worry Workbook: The Cognitive Behavioral Solution by D. A. Clark and A. T. Beck (Guilford Press, 2011)

Freedom from Obsessive-Compulsive Disorder: A Personalized Recovery Program for Living with Uncertainty by J. Grayson (New Harbinger Publications, 2006)

Get Out of Your Mind and Into Your Life: The New Acceptance and Commitment Therapy by S. C. Hayes (New Harbinger Publications, 2005)

Is Fred in the Refrigerator?: Taming OCD and Reclaiming My Life by S. Nicely (New Harbinger Publications, 2018)

Needing to Know for Sure: A CBT-Based Guide to Overcoming Compulsive Checking and Reassurance Seeking by M. N. Seif and S. M. Winston (New Harbinger Publications, 2018)

Obsessed: A Memoir of My Life with OCD by A. Britz (Per Capita Publishing, 2016)

The OCD Answer Book: Professional Answers to More Than 250 Top Questions About Obsessive-Compulsive Disorder by P. McGrath (New Harbinger Publications, 2008)

The OCD Travel Guide: Finding Your Way in a World Full of Risk, Discomfort, and Uncertainty by M. Parker (New Harbinger Publications, 2018)

Rewind, Replay, Repeat: A Memoir of Obsessive-Compulsive Disorder by J. Bell (Atria Books, 2007)

Stop Obsessing!: How to Overcome Your Obsessions and Compulsions by E. B. Foa and R. Wilson (Da Capo Press, 2001)

REFERENCES

This book rests on the body of research conducted by the IOCDF as well as many university programs. The following texts have been critical to my own understanding of OCD and the development of the concepts in this workbook.

Abramowitz, J. S. *The Family Guide to Getting Over OCD: Reclaim Your Life and Help Your Loved One*. New Harbinger Publications, 2019.

Brem, S., E. Grünblatt, R. Drechsler, P. Riederer, and S. Walitza. "The Neurobiological Link Between OCD and ADHD." *ADHD Attention Deficit and Hyperactivity Disorders* 6, no. 3 (2014): 175–202. pmc.ncbi.nlm.nih.gov/articles/PMC4148591.

Granet, S. *The Complete OCD Workbook: A Step-by-Step Guide to Free Yourself from Intrusive Thoughts and Compulsive Behaviors*. Rockridge Press, 2021.

Harris, M. "The Pink Elephant Problem." *Letters from Your Therapist* (blog). *Psychology Today*, July 5, 2023. psychologytoday.com/us/blog/letters-from-your-therapist/202303/the-pink-elephant-problem.

Hershfield, J. *When a Family Member Has OCD: Mindfulness and Cognitive Behavioral Skills to Help Families Affected by Obsessive-Compulsive Disorder*. New Harbinger Publications, 2019.

Hershfield, J., and T. Corboy. *The Mindfulness Workbook for OCD: A Guide to Overcoming Obsessions and Compulsions Using Mindfulness and Cognitive Behavioral Therapy*. New Harbinger Publications, 2019.

Lebowitz, E. R. *Breaking Free of Child Anxiety and OCD: A Scientifically Proven Program for Parents*. New Harbinger Publications, 2019.

Martin, A. F., A. Jassi, A. E. Cullen, M. Broadbent, J. Downs, and G, Krebs. "Co-Occurring Obsessive-Compulsive Disorder and Autism Spectrum Disorder in Young People: Prevalence, Clinical Characteristics and Outcomes." *European Child and Adolescent Psychiatry* 29 (2020): 1603-11. pmc.ncbi.nlm.nih.gov/articles/PMC7595977.

Overbeek, T., K. Schruers, E. Vermetten, and E. Griez. "Comorbidity of Obsessive-Compulsive Disorder and Depression: Prevalence, Symptom Severity, and Treatment Effect." *The Journal of Clinical Psychiatry* 63, no. 12 (2002): 1106-12. pubmed.ncbi.nlm.nih.gov/12523869.

Pittman, C. M., and W. H. Youngs. *Rewire Your OCD Brain: Powerful Neuroscience-Based Skills to Break Free from Obsessive Thoughts and Fears*. New Harbinger Publications, 2021.

Quinlan, K. *The Self-Compassion Workbook for OCD: Lean into Your Fear, Manage Difficult Emotions, and Focus on Recovery*. New Harbinger Publications, 2020.

Schwartz, J. M. *Brain Lock (Twentieth Anniversary Edition): Free Yourself from Obsessive-Compulsive Behavior*. Harper One, 2010.

Winston, S. M., and M. N. Seif. *Overcoming Unwanted Intrusive Thoughts: A CBT-Based Guide to Getting Over Frightening, Obsessive, or Disturbing Thoughts*. New Harbinger Publications, 2021.

INDEX

E

F

P

R

S

ACKNOWLEDGMENTS

I am grateful to the team who discovered my Instagram account and extended an invitation to join this project. As a first-time author, I feel honored that they took a chance on me. My brilliant editor, Clara Song Lee, created the core of this workbook. The clarity and specificity of her guidelines kept my chaotic brain organized and helped me bring this book to life. I would also like to thank my Maine coons, Nadia and Apollo, who diligently started knocking items off my bedstand at 5 a.m. every day. I wrote most of this book in the quiet hours before anyone else needed me.

ABOUT THE AUTHOR

Natalia Aíza, LPC, MA, is the founder of Kairos Wellness Collective, a family-focused OCD and anxiety clinic located in Boulder, Colorado. Over the past three years, Kairos has served more than 2,000 families and individual clients. Natalia is also an advocate for OCD awareness, providing free psychoeducation on her popular Instagram account @letstalk.ocd. Natalia's core mission is to facilitate awareness and healing for individuals with OCD, particularly those who lack access to specialized therapists. Natalia spends her free time trying to convince one of her four teenagers to hang out with her. Visit her at kairoswellnesscollective.com.